The
Rhythm
Of
Resilience

By:
Terri A Senecal

Senecal Music Publishing
645 Solomon Island Rd North
Prince Frederick, MD 20678

Dedication

I would like to dedicate this book to the following people:

GOD

I want to thank God for all my gifts and talents he has given to me

Parents & Family

They always wanted the best for my sisters and me. My parents, Beatrice and Sonny Senecal, always supported me on my musical journey, and I love them for all their support.

My love for my sisters is long and wide. Thank you, Wanda Nephew, who is now in heaven, for your love and support. Penney Senecal who I'm so proud of you. Your support means so much to me.

To the rest of my family, Heather Brier, Corey Nephew, Johnny Nephew, Kerry Miciotto, John Nephew, and all their children and doggies.

Special Support from Friends

Thank you for your support in love and friendship.

Cindy Janke, for 40 years of taking me under your wings and letting me fly with love.

Mera Moon for your love and support, and long hours on the phone.

Chrissy Joy and The Joy Crew

Thank you for blessing my life with love and inspiration.

Pete Sacchetti for believing in me and my abilities.

Sarah Erickson for being so compassionate and loving in my world

And of course, many others…

Bruce Neault, Zad Scott, Pony Baldwin, Alaina & Maddie Posch, Christine Antony, Angela Radivo, Angel (My Sis), The Boyd Family, Sam & Emily Bond, CB, Starbuck Crew in Prince Frederick, Maryland, Kevin Chew, Olivia Ford, Suzanne Kanelopoulos, Suzanne Paulinski, Lisa Laravia and many more…

Cindy Janke

Terri & Beatrice

Terri & Francis Senecal

Terri Senecal & Pete Sacchetti's

John & Wanda Nephew

A songwriter's gift

by Terri A. Senecal

Penney Sencal

Chapter 1
When the Strings Found Me

The Moment the Music Found Me

I remember the exact moment my fingers first touched a guitar string. It's as clear to me now as if it happened yesterday. I was eight years old, aimlessly wandering around the living room, searching for something to fill the quiet afternoon. The house was unusually still, the kind of stillness that makes even a child feel that something different might be on the horizon. Leaning against the far wall was an old acoustic guitar, one that had belonged to someone long before me. No one in the house played it. No one ever talked about it. It was just there, like a forgotten piece of furniture blending into the background. But that day, it wasn't part of the background. It called to me—not literally, of course, but with a pull that was unmistakable, strong enough to stop me in my tracks. Something deeper than curiosity stirred inside me as I stepped toward it, almost as if a part of me knew that this small moment was meant to be important.

When I reached out and brushed a single string, the vibration hummed in the air, flowing through my fingertips. The sound was rough, uneven—a far cry from the smooth notes I would later learn to play—but it didn't matter. It was alive. It was real. It was the first sound I had ever heard that felt like it belonged to me. The vibration lingered even after the tone faded, settling deep within my chest with an unexpected warmth. I couldn't explain it then, but I felt something shift inside me, like I had opened a door I hadn't known existed. That one imperfect note sparked an awareness within me, one that made me stop and listen, wondering what might come next.

In that moment, music didn't feel like something I had just discovered. It felt like something that had been waiting for me—patiently waiting for eight years until I was ready. The sense of familiarity surprised me. How could something I had barely touched feel so natural? I didn't fully understand it at the time, but I recognized the softness it left inside me. It felt like meeting a part of myself that I didn't know existed, but immediately recognized. There was an odd comfort in how the guitar seemed to fit into my hands, even though I didn't know where to place my fingers or how to hold it properly. I wasn't hesitant or intimidated. Instead, it felt as though I was being invited into something, as if the music had simply stepped forward and claimed its place in my life.

From that moment on, I practiced without being told to, without anyone encouraging me to do so. I practiced because something inside me insisted. I didn't think of it as practice—I only knew that every free moment pulled me back to that guitar. I would sit with it for hours, fumbling through sounds, trying to make sense of the patterns I heard. I didn't have a teacher to show me the correct technique or a book to tell me which notes went together. All I had was curiosity and an almost magnetic connection to the instrument. When I discovered two notes that sounded good together, I would repeat them endlessly, trying to understand why they pleased my ears. When I encountered a sound, I didn't like, I shifted my hand and searched again. Without any formal instruction, I learned through trial, instinct, and repetition.

There was something grounding about those early attempts. I wasn't trying to be good at anything. I wasn't trying to impress anyone. I was simply drawn to the sounds the guitar made and how those sounds made me feel. Even when my fingers ached or my strumming sounded choppy, the desire to keep going never waned. It was as though my hands and my heart were learning together, discovering music in sync. With each new sound I managed to create, I could feel my confidence growing. Even the smallest accomplishments felt meaningful. When I finally made my first clean chord, the thrill of hearing it ring out clearly made me want to keep playing.

My parents noticed something different in me when I played. They saw that the guitar drew out a focus in me that they hadn't seen before. I wasn't restless or distracted during practice. I was steady, calm, and intent on making the instrument respond to me. They saw my face change—how concentrated I became, how peaceful I looked, and how completely absorbed I was in the process. I wasn't a particularly outspoken child, but the guitar gave me a way to express things I didn't yet have the words for. My parents recognized that this wasn't just a passing phase or a fleeting interest. It was something that had sparked a fire inside me.

They didn't push me or try to steer my passion. They didn't schedule lessons or pressure me to perform. They simply let me explore it freely, and that made all the difference. Their quiet support created an environment where I could grow without fear of judgment. They didn't treat it as a novelty or a toy. They let me take it seriously. Without realizing it, they had set the stage for music to become more than an interest—it became a refuge, a practice, and, eventually, a purpose.

I spent hours teaching myself chords by ear, unaware that they were even called chords. I would sit cross-legged on the living room floor, pressing my fingers into shapes that felt natural, adjusting them when something didn't sound right. Sometimes, I would experiment by moving a single finger across the fretboard, testing each new sound to see how it changed the tone. I didn't know musicians trained their ears to recognize notes. I didn't realize I was doing something that many people struggled to learn through formal lessons. I simply trusted my ear, knowing that some sounds felt right and others didn't. Slowly, through repetition, I began to recognize patterns. The more I listened, the more I heard. Notes that once seemed random began to connect. Sounds that once felt accidental started to make sense.

There was no formal structure to how I learned, but every attempt carried meaning. I was building a foundation without realizing it. The guitar became my companion, my escape, and the place where I felt fully myself. Even at eight years old, I knew the instrument was offering me something important. It wasn't just teaching me music—it was revealing a part of me I was meant to become. The more time I spent with the strings, the more I realized that music wasn't just something I enjoyed—it was something that shaped me. It gave me identity. It gave me belonging. And though I couldn't have explained it then, I knew that the simple act of touching that first guitar string had opened the door to the rest of my life.

Where I Belonged

I realized music felt like a place I belonged long before I had the words to explain it. As a child, I couldn't articulate why certain moments felt more like home than others, but when I picked up my guitar, I could feel it in my bones. It wasn't just the act of playing; it was the way everything else seemed to fade away when I held it. Time softened. The noise of the world dimmed. I wasn't trying to figure out where I fit in the world—I had already found it. Music wasn't just a hobby or a fun discovery; it was a space that welcomed me exactly as I was.

At eight years old, I didn't fully grasp how rare that feeling could be. All I knew was that when I played, I didn't feel small or uncertain. I felt grounded. I felt full.

At school, kids were surprised someone my age could play. They didn't know I had spent hours alone, practicing in quiet corners of the house, repeating the same chords over and over until my fingers moved without hesitation. Most of them had never seen a kid carry a guitar into the classroom or hum original melodies under their breath during recess. That made me different, and being different came with mixed reactions. Some kids were curious, even impressed. Others didn't know what to make of it and kept their distance.

I wasn't the most outgoing child, and music gave me something to share when words didn't come easily. I wasn't trying to stand out, but the guitar made me visible in a way I hadn't experienced before.

I noticed how people paid attention when I played—even when they didn't say anything. A few teachers asked about my guitar. One even let me bring it to class during a project, where I played a simple melody in front of the class. I was nervous at first, but once I started, something changed. My nerves faded into focus, and for the first time, I saw how music could create a connection between me and others. It didn't erase the awkwardness of being different, but it gave me a confidence I hadn't found anywhere else. I was doing something that felt true, and that truth gave me a quiet strength. It didn't matter if I was the most popular or outgoing; I had something real. That was enough.

Before I even understood the rules of songwriting, I began writing melodies. They came to me in pieces—sometimes as a hum while walking home from school, other times as simple notes I played over and over until they turned into something recognizable. I didn't sit down and decide to write a song. It just happened. The guitar would speak a certain sound, and my hands would follow. The melodies were born from emotion, not structure. I didn't think about keys or bridges or verses—I was simply chasing feelings, following them wherever they led.

Sometimes the melodies had words, and other times they didn't. When they did, the lyrics often reflected whatever I was trying to work through emotionally—uncertainties I couldn't explain, hopes I couldn't name. Songwriting gave me a way to make sense of things I couldn't articulate directly. I would sit on my bed, guitar resting on my legs, letting my fingers move until something new emerged. I didn't know then that I was creating original work. I didn't know that songwriting could become a form of storytelling or therapy. I just knew that the more I played, the more I had to say—even if I didn't speak a word.

That guitar became my safe space. When I felt overwhelmed or unsure of myself, I would reach for it. It became the place where I could sort through my thoughts without judgment or interruption.

I didn't need to explain myself to anyone; I just needed to play. Whether the world felt too loud, too confusing, or too heavy, the moment I held the guitar, everything settled. It wasn't just the music that comforted me—it was the consistency of having something I could return to, something that made sense when everything else didn't. That sense of stability became vital. The guitar was more than an instrument—it was an anchor.

I remember afternoons when I'd come home from school, feeling like I didn't quite fit anywhere. But within minutes of picking up my guitar, that feeling would disappear. The music didn't ask me to be anything other than myself. I didn't have to win anyone over or explain what I was feeling. I could just sit down and play, and in doing so, I found relief. The tension of trying to navigate the world at that age often melted into the chords I strummed. It gave me a way to move through moments that might have otherwise felt stuck. I didn't know how to label those emotions, but I didn't need to. The guitar knew.

Even when I struggled, I never felt discouraged by the effort. If I couldn't get a chord right or a melody didn't sound the way I wanted, I didn't give up. I tried again. And then again. Each failure became a doorway, not a dead end. That quiet persistence shaped the way I approached more than just music—it shaped how I began to handle life. I learned that working through challenges, even the small ones, could lead to breakthroughs. The guitar was teaching me lessons far beyond music theory. It was teaching me patience, resilience, and the value of staying with something when it didn't come easily.

Those early songs—simple, sometimes clumsy—came from a place of raw emotion. They weren't polished or technically impressive, but they were honest. I wasn't trying to sound like anyone else. I was just trying to translate what I felt into sound. In some ways, those first attempts were the purest expressions I've ever created. There was no self-consciousness, no pressure—just the act of creating something new out of nothing. That process gave me permission to explore, to be imperfect, and to express myself without filters.

Looking back, I realize how formative those moments were. They laid the foundation for everything that would follow. I didn't know then that music would carry me through some of the most defining experiences of my life. I didn't understand that this creative outlet would eventually become a calling. But in those early days, playing quietly in my room, writing melodies that no one else would hear, I was building something real. Something that mattered. Something that belonged to me.

Speaking Without Fear

I discovered early on that music gave me a kind of confidence I didn't have anywhere else. I wasn't the boldest child. I didn't raise my hand first in class or volunteer to be the center of attention. I preferred quiet spaces and safe conversations—ones that didn't expose how unsure I sometimes felt inside. But the moment I picked up my guitar, something shifted. It was as though all the noise of self-doubt fell away, leaving behind something steady and sure. The guitar gave me a way to stand taller without speaking louder. I didn't need to become someone else—I just needed to play. In that space, confidence didn't feel forced or performed. It felt honest. It felt like truth.

Playing music silenced the parts of me that constantly questioned whether I was good enough or capable enough. With every note, I proved something to myself—not in a showy or boastful way, but through quiet, personal victories that only I needed to see. I noticed the difference in how I carried myself whenever I had the guitar in my hands. My posture changed. My presence shifted. I wasn't trying to impress anyone; I simply felt more like myself. Over time, that feeling began to spill into other parts of my life. I started walking into rooms with more ease, answering questions with less hesitation, and trusting my own voice more than I had before. The strength I found through music didn't stay confined to practice sessions or performances. It slowly shaped how I saw the world and how I saw myself within it.

One of the first people to notice this transformation was one of my teachers. She wasn't a music teacher—just a classroom instructor who cared enough to look beneath the surface. She paid attention to the way I lit up whenever I talked about the guitar. She noticed how I focused differently on days when I'd been practicing before school. One afternoon, after class, she pulled me aside and asked if I would consider bringing my guitar in for a class presentation. At first, I hesitated. I wasn't sure I was ready to share that part of myself in front of my peers. But there was something in her tone—gentle, encouraging, and sincere—that gave me the confidence to say yes.

When the day came, I stood at the front of the classroom with my guitar resting against my shoulder. My hands trembled slightly as I adjusted the strap, and my heart raced faster than I wanted it to. But when I strummed the first chord, the nerves began to fade. I wasn't performing—I was sharing. That difference mattered. When I finished, the class applauded politely, but it was her smile I noticed first. She nodded, affirming not just what I had played, but the courage it took to stand there. That moment stayed with me. She didn't just offer praise—she gave me belief. Her encouragement became a mirror, reflecting back a version of myself I hadn't fully recognized yet.

That single experience opened the door to others. I began playing small pieces at family gatherings. They weren't elaborate performances—just simple songs played in living rooms or during holiday dinners. I felt nervous every time. My hands would sweat, and my chest would tighten before the first note. But once I started playing, the fear softened into something else—something closer to joy. I watched relatives lean in, their faces relaxing as the music filled the room. Even when I stumbled on a chord or forgot a lyric, no one seemed to mind. In those moments, music became a bridge between me and the people I loved. It gave me a way to connect without relying on bold words or confident conversation. It asked only that I be present, honest, and willing to let the sound speak where I might have stayed silent.

I slowly began to understand that music wasn't just something I did—it was a language I could speak without fear. That realization changed everything. I had never felt fluent in the usual ways people connected. I wasn't someone who dominated conversations or took up space easily. But music gave me another way in. It allowed me to express emotions I didn't yet have names for. It let me say things I didn't know how to say out loud. The strings became my sentences. The melodies became my message. And people listened—not always with applause, but with attention. That attention made me feel seen in a way nothing else ever had.

As I continued playing, I noticed how creativity helped me feel recognized—not so much by others, but by myself. It was like uncovering another layer of who I was, one that had been there all along, quiet but undeniable. Writing songs, experimenting with rhythms, trying new chord progressions—these weren't just musical exercises. They were acts of self-discovery. I was uncovering parts of myself I hadn't known existed. There was power in shaping something from nothing, in turning a feeling or idea into a sound that could be shared. I began to understand that this wasn't about talent or performance. It was about identity.

Each time I finished writing a melody or played something I hadn't mastered before, I felt a subtle but powerful recognition—not the kind that needed validation, but the kind that quietly said, yes, this is who I am. That internal affirmation mattered more than applause or approval ever could. It grounded me. Creativity became a mirror that didn't distort or demand. It reflected back my truth—unpolished, evolving, and real.

I also noticed how creating music brought me a deep sense of peace. Even when a song was incomplete or a melody didn't come out the way I wanted, the process itself was comforting. The structure of music—the repetition, the rhythm, the steady pursuit of harmony—gave shape to emotions that might have otherwise felt overwhelming or undefined. Within that shape, I found clarity.

I didn't need to fully understand what I was feeling. I only needed to play. And through playing, those feelings stretched out, softened, and revealed themselves in their own time.

That discovery stayed with me. It taught me that my voice didn't have to sound like anyone else's to matter. I didn't need to follow the path others expected or seek attention in traditional ways. My gift had its own rhythm and its own way of emerging. As long as I honored that rhythm—by showing up, creating honestly, and staying true to myself—I knew I was on the right path. Music wasn't just something I loved. It was something that loved me back—quietly, steadily, and without condition.

In the years to come, this understanding would become a compass. It would remind me who I was when the noise of life tried to tell me otherwise. It would keep me grounded when disappointment threatened to shake my foundation. And it all began here, with the realization that music was more than sound. It was a lifeline—a way to be known, not only by the world, but by myself.

The First Door

I didn't know it at the time, but music would shape every stage of my life. At eight years old, I wasn't thinking about legacy or calling. I wasn't worrying about where anything might lead. I was simply following a sound that made me feel real. I didn't need a future mapped out—I just needed a guitar in my lap. But looking back now, I can see how every small step I took back then quietly moved me forward. Every note I played, every song I hummed, every chord I learned by instinct was doing more than building skill. It was building something deeper. What started as a pastime slowly became a path. Without realizing it, I was stepping into a lifelong pursuit that would define who I was, how I thought, and what I believed I was created to do.

Music wasn't just part of my routine; it became the lens through which I understood everything else. When I felt confused, I turned to the guitar. When I felt overwhelmed, I wrote melodies. When I was joyful, I played louder. Music became my first response—my default, my way of making sense of the world. Other kids leaned into sports or social circles. I leaned into strings. I wasn't trying to escape life; I was trying to understand it. And every time I picked up the guitar, the world felt a little clearer, a little more manageable.

I began dreaming about talent shows long before I ever signed up for one. At night, I would lie in bed imagining myself standing on a stage. I pictured the lights, the quiet anticipation in the room, the sound of my own breathing as I walked out with a guitar in my hands. My heart would be pounding. I didn't imagine fame or trophies. I imagined the music filling the space and connecting me to people who truly heard it. These weren't fantasies about grandeur. They were glimpses of possibility. Even at that young age, I felt something pulling me forward. It wasn't pressure—it was potential. And with every dream, the idea of sharing my music publicly shifted from a distant "maybe someday" into a quiet but certain "when I'm ready."

Those dreams stayed private. I didn't announce them or talk about them out loud. But they became part of how I saw myself. They gave me motivation. They influenced how I practiced and how I showed up for the instrument. I wasn't just playing to pass the time—I was preparing, building something I couldn't yet fully name. I practiced in front of mirrors, not to perfect movements or appearances, but to grow comfortable in my own presence. I wanted to know what it felt like to be seen and heard for who I really was. That desire—to be known through music—settled in quietly, but it rooted itself deeply.

My parents played a significant role during that time. They never forced music on me, and they never tried to live through what I was doing. They simply noticed how much it mattered. Instead of pressure, they offered respect. Instead of expectations, they offered balance. School still came first. Rest still mattered. Chores didn't disappear. But within those boundaries, they gave me freedom—freedom to grow, freedom to explore, freedom to fail and try again.

They didn't hover, but they paid attention. They didn't micromanage, but they were present. When I broke a string, they helped me replace it. When I wanted to learn a song I heard on the radio, they encouraged me to figure it out on my own. They didn't overpraise my progress, and they didn't criticize my mistakes. Their support was calm and consistent. And that consistency gave me room to become. I wasn't playing to earn approval—I already had it. Their belief in me was quiet, but it was solid. And within that stability, I felt safe to keep going.

That balance—freedom paired with grounding—allowed me to continue when I might have otherwise quit. On days when my fingers hurt or progress felt slow, I never questioned whether music was worth it. I knew it was. And I knew my parents believed that, too. That unspoken understanding gave me courage. It showed me that I didn't have to choose between being responsible and being creative. I could be both. That realization stayed with me and became a principle I would carry into adulthood.

With that support surrounding me, I began imagining a future where music wasn't just something I did—it was everything. I started seeing myself as a songwriter, as a performer, as someone who might one day walk into a studio and create something lasting. I imagined albums with my name on them, not because I wanted fame, but because I wanted to contribute something meaningful. I dreamed of collaborating with others who loved music the way I did, of building something bigger than myself. It wasn't about recognition. It was about purpose.

I didn't know how I would get there. I didn't understand what it would require or how long the journey might take. But I knew what it felt like to play a song and sense something shift inside me. I knew the peace that came from finishing a melody that had lived in my head for days. I knew the connection that happened when someone listened to a song I had written and said, "That's exactly how I feel." And I wanted more of that. I wanted to wake up every day doing work that made people feel understood.

As I imagined that future, I started setting quiet, personal goals. Learn three new chords this month. Write one original song by the end of the semester. Record myself playing and listen back to improve. These weren't assignments or obligations—they were mile markers. Each one brought me a step closer to something I could almost reach. I didn't have a detailed plan. I had a feeling. A pull. A rhythm. And I trusted it enough to follow.

What I didn't realize then was that all of those moments—playing alone in my room, imagining stages, talking with my parents about new songs—were preparing me for something larger. They weren't just childhood memories. They were the roots of a calling. And without knowing it, I was answering that call one small choice at a time.

That eight-year-old version of me, sitting cross-legged with a guitar too big for her arms, opened the first door to the rest of her life. She didn't have a strategy or a timeline. She didn't have a clear definition of success. But she had instinct. She had drive. She had a voice just beginning to take shape. And she had the courage to follow where it led.

There's something powerful about beginnings that don't announce themselves. There were no trumpets when I strummed my first chord. No applause. No audience at all. But that quiet moment became the starting line for everything that followed. I didn't know it then, but that was when everything shifted—not because I played perfectly, but because I played honestly.

That honesty became the through-line of my story. It grounded me when the journey became difficult. It reminded me who I was when other voices tried to tell me otherwise. And it always pointed me back to a simple truth: music wasn't something I chose. It chose me. And from the moment I said yes—without even realizing I was saying it—my life began moving in rhythm with something far greater than myself.

Wanda, Beatrice & Terri Senecal

Wanda & Terri Senecal

Chapter 2
The Stage Became My Classroom

Where The Lights First Found Me

Talent shows quickly became my identity, long before I had the awareness or vocabulary to articulate myself. Up until that point, most of my musical persona was shaped privately—inside my room, in quiet corners of the house, within the safety of practice sessions no one else witnessed, basically free from judgment. But my first talent show performance marked the moment my music stepped out of those private spaces and became something I shared with the world. I didn't enter these shows with expectations to discover anything exceptional about myself. I just had fire in my heart, which was to perform and let the music bring the change in the world that it had brought to me. Yet, the experience became the beginning of a lifelong realization: the stage was not an escape from who I was—it was a mirror reflecting truths I couldn't see anywhere else.

The first time I stepped onto a stage, the space felt bigger than anything I had encountered. The atmosphere buzzed lightly with conversations, at once familiar and unfamiliar—classmates, parents, and teachers, each waiting for the show to begin. Chairs scraped the floor as people settled in, stage crew members whispered instructions to one another, and somewhere in the distance, a microphone hummed with feedback. I felt the electricity of anticipation thick in the air, but nothing could comprehend the feeling of the moment I was called forward. When my name was announced, it felt as though the world paused for a moment before everything shifted into focus. My hands trembled slightly as I held my guitar, but I walked confidently toward the light because something inside me was sure that I belonged there.

Standing on stage made me feel more alive than I did anywhere else. It wasn't just the brightness of the spotlight or the quiet expectancy of the audience—it was the sense of universal alignment that washed over me the moment I began to play. Each note seemed to expand inside the room, creating a connection between me and everyone listening. At that moment, I didn't feel small, overwhelmed, or unsure. The anxieties that followed me through everyday life faded when I was under the spotlight. My voice, my instrument, and my presence blended into something larger than fear or doubt, which I had left behind me. I felt grounded in a way I couldn't achieve anywhere else. It was as though the stage drew out the fullest, truest version of myself.

That feeling only got bigger when I participated in more shows. With each performance, I became increasingly aware that the stage had become an unexpected form of guidance and gratitude for me. It taught me what confidence really felt like. It taught me how to trust myself. And perhaps most importantly, it reassured me that the parts of myself that I was so unsure of were the same parts that could settle and take shape. Every time, I could feel my nerves shoot up before my performance, but the moment I stepped into the lights, those nerves turned into art. The stage opened me up to an environment where I learned to breathe, center myself, and be my true self in ways I couldn't replicate anywhere else.

The surprising part was that I kept winning. Win after win, show after show, my name was called. Yet every win surprised me. Not because I believed I wasn't capable, but because I hadn't walked on the stage expecting victory. I wasn't there to do my best, not knowing that I was the best. Neither was I performing to defeat anyone. I wasn't fueled by applause or driven by competition. In my head, everyone is fully capable of doing what they do best. In all sincerity, I performed because I loved to play and wanted to share what music gave me. Each time I placed first, I felt a wave of disbelief wash over me—not the kind that questions worthiness, but the kind that reflects genuine humility. Every win felt like something that happened around me, not something I demanded from the experience.

Even though the thought of winning didn't fuel my motivation, I still found myself paying close attention to every competitor. I deeply studied each performer—not out of jealousy, but out of curiosity and appreciation for everyone's effort. I wanted to understand what made their performances stand out. I noticed how some contestants walked confidently onto the stage, how others encouraged themselves before beginning, and how a few seemed to forget the audience entirely once they started performing. Every performer had a distinct presence, and I watched them closely because they taught me something about art, courage, and individuality. Observing them became part of my learning process, and I did learn a lot.

While some performers seemed competitive, I saw how unique everyone was. Each contestant had their own story, and each song choice came with some personal relevance. I paid attention to how they moved, how they played, how they connected with the audience—or didn't. Watching others in their form allowed me to see performance as an art that extended beyond the voice or instrument. It included the emotional energy every performer carried, the subtle choices they made, and the way they held themselves even after the last note faded. The more I watched, the more I learned. And the more I learned, the more deeply I felt drawn to performing.

Through these observations, I realized that performing required vulnerability. It wasn't enough to play well or sing clearly. Performance demanded honesty and really putting yourself out there in the open. The stage required me to reveal a part of myself, even when I wasn't sure how it would be received. That realization didn't intimidate me—it enlightened me. As an artist, vulnerability was never about a weakness; it was the doorway through which real connection flowed. When I stepped on stage, I wasn't just hiding behind talent. I was finally offering something meaningful. I understood that people weren't only listening to the music—they were listening to the person playing it, and I, as a performer, had the power to flow through my heart. They were responding to the emotion, intention, and truth that I would transfer through my music. That understanding shaped the way I approached each performance.

The stage taught me a kind of courage that didn't just depend on perfection. Mistakes happened, that's completely natural. Notes sometimes wobbled, my voice occasionally cracked, but each time, I kept playing, which meant that my showing up mattered the most. And in doing so, I learned that the heart of performing wasn't flawless execution—it was transparency and showing the world that I am as human as everyone else. As grounded as I am in my talent, it's rooted in reality and effort. With practice and a belief in yourself, you can reach excellence. It was the willingness to share real emotion, whether confident or trembling. I learned that showing up mattered more than showing off. And because of that, the stage became a place where I could grow without fear of failing.

As I continued performing, I saw that each time I stepped into the spotlight, I got closer to a version of myself, more aware of who I was becoming. The stage wasn't simply a platform—it was a teacher. It taught me resilience by pushing me to keep going even when I was clouded with doubts. It taught me humility by reminding me that I was part of something larger than applause or awards. And most importantly, it taught me that music wasn't something separate from the rest of my life—it was woven into the very core of my very being.

Every performance opened a new layer of myself. Every chord I strummed felt like a new declaration of identity. And every time I walked off the stage, I carried a deeper understanding of my own voice with me—it was beyond the sounds, but the purpose behind it. Those early experiences didn't just teach me how to perform— they taught me how to live with intention, honesty, and courage.

By the time I completed my first few talents shows, it was pretty much accepted that the stage wasn't a performance ground anymore, but more like a classroom unlike any other. It helped me uncover aspects of myself that would have stayed hidden if I hadn't dared to step into the light. And each time I returned to that light, the lessons got deeper. It wasn't about trophies. It wasn't about recognition. It was about awakening, derived from a divine calling. It was about standing in a place that demanded presence, truth, and vulnerability—and discovering that those qualities were already within me, waiting to be activated and unleash my true self.

Lessons Behind The Applause

Applause surely fueled me, but it was never the reason behind my fire. The sound of crowds, the brief wave of cheers, the nods of recognition—they all offered a kind of positive affirmation, but they weren't the reward for me. They weren't what pulled me to the stage, and they never dictated my desire to return. The absolute satisfaction came from knowing that I had delivered something from my heart. When I walked off the stage after a performance, what stayed with me wasn't how loud the audience got, but whether I had expressed the music the way it needed to be heard. The applause was a moment. The connection I felt through the music was long-lasting.

As I got more involved in talent shows, I noticed how applause affected different contestants. For some, it was everything—the measure of success, the reason to compete, the validation they sought. For me, it served as a checkpoint, not a destination, and I don't want to compare, but I think this is where most people go wrong, they seek validation. For me, the crowd was feedback and a source of positive affirmation, but mostly, I was always reminded of how it left an impact that was way bigger than the validation. The audience reminded me that I will be heard. But even in the silence between songs or the scattered claps from a small audience, I found value. It reminded me that the stage wasn't just a place for recognition—it was a place for offering, and I was willing to offer. I was offering my voice, my story, and my truth. And sometimes, that mattered more in a quiet reception than in a thunderous response.

Long before I understood the term "stage presence," I was learning about it in the process. I didn't know there was a name for the ability to hold space with your posture, your gaze, your energy. I just knew that how I carried myself when I walked onto the stage mattered. The moment I stepped into the light, people formed impressions—before I even chimed a note or opened my mouth to sing. I learned to walk calmly, to center myself, to plant my feet with the right intention. I paid attention to how I held the guitar, how I looked into the crowd, how I moved, or didn't move. These weren't rehearsed techniques taught in a workshop—they were habits formed through attention and reflection that I had acquired with experience.

I began to recognize that every part of a performance told a story, beyond the music. The silence before the first note, the transitions between verses, the way I breathed between lyrics—all of it contributed to an insightful message. The way I stood and communicated confidence or uncertainty. The way I bowed or exited left a lasting impression. Without knowing it, I was building a presence that extended way above my voice. I was learning how to create an experience, not just deliver a song. And every time I stepped onto that stage, I refined that presence, one moment at a time.

Behind the curtain, my parents were my quiet backstage crew who really supported me. They didn't shout instructions or fuss over my performance. They weren't stage parents pushing for perfection either. Instead, they offered real support. They were the ones making sure my guitar was tuned on time, that I had time to warm up, and that I took care of the urgencies if I had left any spaces behind. Their presence was steady, not loud. And in their steadiness, I found reassurance. I never felt pressured to win or outperform. They never made the spotlight feel like a weight.

They reminded me that I was loved, whether I played flawlessly or fumbled my way through.

Before each show, I'd find them in the audience—never front row, never drawing attention. Just there like a guardian angel watching and supporting me. Watching with eyes that didn't expect, but believed, and I must accept that this belief was the most significant support for me. Their quiet confidence in me allowed me to approach each performance with a clear mind. I didn't perform for them, but knowing they were there gave me a sense of responsibility. It reminded me that no matter what happened on stage, there was a place I could return to where I was understood and accepted, regardless of my performance.

One person, however, played a pivotal role in strengthening my confidence during those early performances: my mentor. While she wasn't directly involved in the talent shows, her encouragement profoundly shaped how I approached them. She saw something in me beyond the music— something grounded, reflective, and worth nurturing. She asked thoughtful questions about my songs, listened with sincere interest, and offered constructive feedback rather than criticism. Her voice—soft yet resolute—reminded me that talent is something to be cultivated, not merely applauded.

She created space for conversations about nerves, about process, and about the unseen aspects of performing. And when doubt crept in—whether over a song choice, a missed note, or an imperfect performance—she brought perspective. She never demanded perfection. Instead, she highlighted my moments of growth. I guess that's where I learned never to compare myself, but to do my best every time. That outlook allowed me to improve without self-judgment. Through her support, I learned to believe in myself not just when things went well, but when they didn't. That belief became a powerful part of my internal narrative. Her faith in me helped build the foundation of my self-confidence.

One lesson I learned early and often was how much work went into a three-minute song. What appeared effortless on stage was the result of hours of behind-the-scenes preparation. Selecting the right song was just the first step. I'd spend days rehearsing, fine-tuning, adjusting phrasing, and polishing dynamics. I rehearsed endlessly, trying to make each note sound intentional. Sometimes the melody chimed easily, other times I'd rework entire sections until they felt right. I experimented with tempo, explored different keys, and occasionally reworked the arrangement to better match my voice or convey the song's message.

The details mattered. Transitions between verses, the timing of a pause, the emphasis on a single word—each demanded careful consideration. Rehearsals were far from glamorous. They were often quiet, repetitive, and physically demanding. My fingers would ache. My voice would get tired. There were moments of frustration, moments when I considered abandoning the song and starting from scratch. Yet through it all, I learned commitment. I came to understand that strong performances don't happen by chance; they are built through intention, patience, and persistence.

Recognizing the effort behind each performance deepened my respect for the process. It instilled a sense of discipline unlike anything I had experienced before. I couldn't show up unprepared and expect the same outcome. I had to invest the time, make deliberate choices, and commit to repetition until everything felt instinctive. This wasn't solely just about technical ability—it was about respect. Respect for the music, for the audience, and for myself. That mindset extended into every area of my life. I began approaching school, relationships, and personal challenges with the same dedication I brought to the stage. Performing was shaping me far beyond its physical space.

Each performance, though brief in length, carried weight. Every one of them contained hours of unseen effort—practice sessions, revisions, self-doubt, and breakthroughs. When I finally stepped onstage, the audience witnessed a polished result. What they didn't see was the journey it took to get there. But I saw it. And over time, I grew to value the invisible work even more than the visible outcome. It made me appreciate the beauty of process, the resilience built through repetition, and the silent power of preparation.

Even when nerves threatened undo all that preparation moments before a performance, I learned to channel that anxious energy into focus. I discovered how to ground myself in the music, allowing the familiar rhythm of the song to steady my racing thoughts. I didn't pretend the nerves weren't there. I acknowledged them, breathed through them, and used them as fuel. That shift—from fear into forward motion—became one of the most valuable lessons the stage ever taught me.

Courage In The Spotlight

I learned to manage nerves and convert them into energy. At first, the anxiety I felt before stepping on stage threatened to consume me. My stomach would twist, my hands would sweat, and my thoughts would spiral. It was a familiar wave that crashed every time I stood in the wings waiting to be called. But with each performance, I stopped resisting the nerves and began understanding them. They weren't a sign of weakness—they were evidence that I cared. That shift in perspective changed everything. Instead of dreading that pre-performance tension, I learned to use it to sharpen my focus. The nerves became fuel, adrenaline that heightened my awareness and grounded me in the moment. They didn't vanish; they evolved.

The more I performed, the more I began to anticipate those sensations. I stopped hoping for calm and instead learned to prepare for the surge of anxiety. I developed rituals— deep breathing, quiet affirmations, gentle stretching—that helped steady both body and mind.

I'd repeat phrases to myself like, "You've done the work," or "Let the music speak."

Those simple words weren't magic, but they created space between fear and performance. They helped me reconnect with my purpose—not to impress, but to express. Over time, I began to welcome the nerves as a companion rather than an enemy. They reminded me that I was about to do something meaningful.

Even when I didn't win, I never walked away discouraged. Losing didn't intimidate me; holding back did. Each time I chose to step on stage, I understood that I was entering a vulnerable position. There was always the risk that the audience wouldn't connect, that the judges wouldn't respond, that I would forget a lyric or strike the wrong chord. Yet none of that ever felt as heavy as the idea of staying silent. Regret never came from losing—it only came from silence, from staying on the sidelines when my heart knew I belonged in the spotlight.

Trying was the true victory. Every time I stepped onto the stage, I had already achieved something meaningful. I had confronted uncertainty, pushed past hesitation, and committed to the work by sharing something genuine. Whether I left with a ribbon or a trophy never diminished the worth of that act. And the more I performed, the more deeply I internalized that truth. Effort carried its own reward. Showing up was a victory. Expression, even in imperfection, held a power all its own.

There were moments when people underestimated me because of my age. I could see it in their expressions when I walked onto the stage—curious glances, polite smiles, tempered expectations. I didn't resent it; in many ways, I understood it. I was small, soft-spoken, and often one of the youngest in the lineup. I didn't appear to be someone who could command a room. But that only made the moment of connection more powerful. When I began to play, and people leaned in, surprised by the sound, I watched perceptions shift. Their focus sharpened. Their posture changed. In those moments, I realized that ability doesn't announce itself through volume or age. It reveals itself through presence, in clarity, in truth.

Being underestimated gave me a quiet kind of strength. I never tried to prove anyone wrong—I simply let the music speak for itself. I didn't step onstage with defensiveness; I stepped on with purpose. Each performance became an opportunity not to impress, but to invite people to see beyond the surface and feel something unexpected. And the more often that happened, the more confident I became— not loudly or showily, but deeply and steadily. Confidence wasn't about being the loudest in the room; it was about being secure in what you carried within you.

When I did win, it wasn't the award that fulfilled me. Victory didn't feel like validation—music itself did. Long before any judge rendered a decision, I knew when I had given my best. I could feel when I had fully connected to the song, when the message had come through clearly, when I had left everything on the stage, that internal knowing meant more to me than any certificate. It was the sense that I had been faithful to the moment. That I had honored the music, the audience, and myself. That feeling lingered far longer with me than any formal recognition.

Sometimes, after a win, people congratulated me as though the result was the most important part. But I defined success differently. I looked back at the effort, the discipline, the emotional depth I had reached, and the growth I had experienced since the last performance. I wasn't chasing first place—I was chasing honesty. And when I delivered a performance that felt true, I carried that pride with me, regardless of what the scoreboard said. That mindset kept me grounded. It reminded me that music was never about proving anything. It was about a far greater offering.

Alongside these performances, I also experienced my first taste of friendly competition. It wasn't cutthroat or aggressive, but there was an energy that pushed all of us to improve. I began to recognize familiar faces at different events—other young performers who were just as passionate, just as committed, just as eager to grow. We shared smiles backstage, exchanged nervous glances, and sometimes offered quiet words of encouragement. There was mutual respect, even admiration. We understood that we were walking the same path, even if our styles differed. That sense of camaraderie made the entire experience richer.

Competition, when rooted in respect, taught me discipline. It pushed me to take my preparation seriously, refine my craft, and delve deeper into the emotions behind the songs I chose. Watching someone else deliver a strong performance didn't intimidate me—it inspired me.

I would ask myself, "What made that so compelling?" and carry those questions back into my own practice.

I wasn't striving to outdo anyone else—I was trying to surpass who I had been before. And being surrounded by others who felt the same way created an environment rooted in growth.

The structure of those events—deadlines, rehearsals, show dates—also gave my development a steady rhythm. I learned to work within timelines, practice consistently, and make intentional decisions. Each performance became a project with a clear beginning, middle, and end. Through that process, I developed habits that extended far beyond the stage. I learned how to manage time, set goals, and push through frustration. Friendly competition had a subtle but powerful way of strengthening me from within.

Looking back, I see how those years shaped me not just as a musician, but as a person. They taught me that courage isn't loud—it's consistent. That confidence isn't boastful—it's steady. That growth doesn't happen by accident—it happens when you show up, again and again, regardless of the outcome. Those lessons were woven into every show, every rehearsal, and every decision to try once more. As I moved forward, they became the foundation for everything that followed.

Foundations In The Footlights

I began developing my own performance style during those early years, though I didn't realize it at the time. When I first started performing, my focus was simply on making it through a song without forgetting lyrics or missing a chord. But with each show, something deeper began to cut through the surface. I started noticing the subtle ways I interacted with my audience—how I tilted my head on specific notes, lingered a little longer on emotionally charged lyrics, and moved my hands as I played. These weren't calculated choices; they were instinctive, shaped by feeling and repetition. Over time, those small gestures grew into something distinctly my own.

It wasn't about creating a polished image. I wasn't trying to be theatrical or adopt a persona. Instead, my style emerged out of honesty. I paid attention to how the songs made me feel and allowed those emotions to guide my movement and expression. If a lyric carried weight, I allowed my expression to shift with it. If the rhythm felt light, I let my body loosen into it. I began to understand that my presence on stage was as much a part of the performance as the music itself. In recognizing that, I started shaping a voice— not just in tone, but in the full experience I offered an audience.

Each performance also taught me how to read the room. I learned to adapt—not by changing the substance of my music, but by how I delivered it. Some audiences leaned in, quiet and reflective. Others were more reactive and vocal in their support. I didn't alter who I was to fit in, but I learned to connect in ways that felt genuine. I found a rhythmic balance between vulnerability and strength, between expression and control. That balance became the foundation of my style—unspoken, but deeply felt.

Talent shows taught me discipline more than anything else I had encountered up to that point. They were fun, yes, but they demanded structure. There were deadlines to meet, material to prepare, nerves to manage, and stamina to sustain. I couldn't just show up and hope for the best. I had to put in the work—really put in the work. Choosing a song meant more than picking something popular. It meant finding something I could connect with deeply enough to carry through nerves, distractions, and expectations. Once the song was chosen, the rehearsal required consistency. I had to run it over and over—not just until I got it right once, but until I could deliver it flawlessly every time.

That kind of discipline didn't come naturally; it had to be cultivated. I had to develop focus when it would've been easier to get distracted. I had to push through days when inspiration felt distant. I had to hold myself accountable, even when no one was watching. But as I committed to the process, I began to notice results—not just in the quality of my performances, but in how I carried myself. Discipline spilled over into other areas of my life. It shaped how I approached schoolwork, friendships, and even daily routines. It became a habit to show up for myself, honor my commitments, and follow through with intention.

Receiving feedback was another unexpected lesson from those early shows. At first, I struggled to interpret the comments I received—whether from judges, teachers, or even peers. Some praised my voice, others pointed out areas for improvement, and occasionally, someone would offer a suggestion that felt difficult to hear. But I quickly learned that feedback wasn't negative criticism—it was a tool. I learned to listen carefully, filtering through the comments to find what would help me grow. I didn't treat every opinion as the absolute truth, but I paid attention to patterns. When multiple people noted the same thing, I took notice. If someone offered insight about delivery, timing, or clarity, I considered how to integrate it into my next rehearsal.

Humility became essential in that process. I had to set aside the desire to hear that I was already exceptional and instead embrace the idea that I could improve. That mindset made me teachable. It allowed me to separate my sense of self from my performance. I could receive critique without letting it shake my confidence, and I could embrace praise without letting it inflate my ego. Feedback became an essential part of my journey—a mirror that showed me more clearly, a gentle push that guided me forward.

One of the most powerful lessons I learned during those years was that performing was more than playing music—it was storytelling. A song wasn't merely a series of chords and lyrics. It was a narrative, a message, an emotional journey. Every time I stood on stage, I wasn't just delivering producing music—I was telling a story. Sometimes it was my own, sometimes it belonged to someone else. But always, without a doubt, it was something that had to be felt and heard. That understanding transformed how I approached each performance.

I started asking myself, "What am I trying to say with this song? What do I want people to walk away with?"

That shift in perspective deepened everything. It made me more intentional in my song selections. I stopped selecting pieces just because they were technically impressive or well-known. I began choosing songs that carried weight—songs that said something meaningful, that revealed a truth I resonated with. I began practicing not just for precision, but also for authenticity. I thought about pacing, silence, and emphasis. I imagined the audience not just as passive spectators, but as participants—people who needed to feel the emotion, follow the story, and leave with a lasting experience.

The storytelling aspect of performing helped me uncover another dimension of myself. I realized I had something to express that held meaning, even when I wasn't writing the lyrics. My interpretation, my delivery, my presence—all of it shaped the story in a way that was uniquely my own. That realization empowered me. It reminded me that I didn't need the perfect words or the perfect stage to share something meaningful. I could do it right there, with the tools I already had, with the voice I was still learning to inhabit fully.

As I look back on those early talent-show years, I see they were never just about music. They were about my formation. Every stage, every performance, every moment of applause or silence, contributed to the foundation that would carry me forward. Those years weren't just preparation for something greater—they were something great in themselves. They instilled in me the resilience to try, the discipline to grow, the humility to learn, and the courage to speak my heart through sound.

They also gave me something more: a sense of belonging. In those rooms, under those lights, I wasn't trying to become someone else—I was becoming more of who I already was. The songs, the nerves, the effort, the stories— they all revealed something more profound. I wasn't just performing. I was taking root. And every chord I played was an echo of that process, a signal that I had found a place where all the parts of me—shy and bold, uncertain and steady—could exist in harmony within myself and my surroundings.

Chapter 3
Nashville Lit a New Fire in Me

Walking Into The Heart Of A Dream

My trip to Nashville felt like stepping into a dream I hadn't yet allowed myself to embrace. For years, I had imagined places where music didn't need explanation—where it wasn't a hobby or a side interest, but the essence of my daily life, my very being. I had heard stories about Nashville, watched performances filmed there, and absorbed bits of its culture through songs that referenced its streets. Still, nothing prepared me for what it felt like, actually, to arrive. As we drove into the city, I pressed my face against the window, wanting to take in every sign, every building, and every detail. It felt like crossing a threshold, leaving ordinary life behind and entering a world built for people specifically like me.

There was an energy in the air the moment I stepped out of the car. The breeze carried sounds I hadn't expected to hear at once: someone strumming on a corner, a harmonica drifting from an alleyway, and the faint echo of a band warming up blocks away. It felt like the city warmly welcomed me with layers of melody before I even reached the main streets. Nashville didn't whisper its identity; it projected with unmistakable clarity. Music wasn't limited to stages or studios—it spilled into everything as if it were the livelihood. Every building seemed to lean toward the sound, as if listening keenly. I stood still for a moment, soaking it in, and realized I had arrived somewhere that made me feel understood without saying a word.

The city pulsed with music at every turn. It wasn't just the famous venues or the iconic spots tourists were attracted to—it was the entire landscape of the atmosphere. Restaurants had small platforms tucked into corners for live performances. Shops played local artists over their speakers as if they believed in the music that resonated with the state's demographic. Even the sidewalks felt like extensions of a stage, where musicians set up without hesitation, performing as naturally as breathing. I'd never been anywhere that embraced creativity so openly, or supported it so naturally. Instead of feeling out of place for wanting to write songs or play guitar, I felt like I had finally found a place where my passion blended effortlessly with everything around me and about me. Here, music wasn't an exception—it was the expectation.

Walking down the streets, I felt an undeniable pull towards everything I encountered. Each doorway beckoned, every song stopped me in my tracks, and I couldn't help but watch every musician who had planted themselves on the pavement, playing with raw, untamed passion. Nashville had a way of breaking down the barriers between performer and listener. It made the act of creating music feel deeply personal and incredibly expansive, intimate yet universal. What struck me most wasn't just the undeniable talent—though it was impossible to overlook—but the sheer dedication. These artists played as if every note held a piece of their soul. Observing them awakened something in me. I understood that this city wasn't just a stop for artists—it was a place they poured themselves into.

Surrounded by that level of creativity, I felt both exhilarated and daunted by the thought of competing. I had signed up for the songwriting competition months before the trip, excited for the opportunity, but unaware of the intensity I would face. When I arrived at the venue, the difference was immediately clear—this wasn't the stage I was familiar with back home. The other competitors carried themselves with a quiet confidence that came not from arrogance, but from experience. Some carried notebooks worn from constant rewriting, others tuned their instruments with practiced precision, and many spoke about previous competitions or collaborations with the casual familiarity of seasoned pros. I watched them closely, feeling the weight of the moment settle deep within.

Yet, the fear didn't push me away—it propelled me forward. I felt as though I was standing on the edge of something truly meaningful, and turning back would have been far more painful than moving ahead. Competing here was like stepping into a room where the stakes were high but the experience was irreplaceable. I knew that if I performed well, it wouldn't be due to luck—it would be because I deserved to stand next to these creatives. After all, I had something genuine to contribute. That realization grounded me, even as nerves threatened to take over.

When it was my turn to perform, I remember walking onto the stage with my heart, the sound of each beat echoing in my ears. The lights above me felt brighter than any I had ever stood under, and the room seemed larger, though it wasn't physically overwhelming. There was an unspoken pressure in the air that came not from intimidation, but from intensity—an unspoken agreement among everyone present that songwriting mattered here. It mattered deeply. I lifted my guitar, took a steady breath, and let the first chord ring out. In that moment, my nerves didn't fade; they shifted, transforming into focus. I felt every lyric with a clarity I hadn't experienced before. I wasn't performing at Nashville—I was performing within it, contributing to the tapestry of music that filled the city.

Winning third place meant more than any trophy I had received before. When my name was called, I wasn't struck with shock or disbelief; instead, I felt profoundly moved. The recognition came from people who understood the craft, people who dedicated their lives to songwriting. Their acknowledgment wasn't casual—it was informed. That made all the difference. It wasn't just that I placed; it was that my work held its own in a city full of people who took music seriously. Third place might have sounded small to some, but to me, it was monumental. It was validation from a place that didn't hand out praise easily.

That moment changed something inside me in a way nothing else had. It proved that my work belonged among real songwriters—not just in theory, but in practice. I had always believed that songwriting was meaningful, but this was proof that it reached beyond my immediate surroundings. It showed me that the songs I wrote in notebooks late at night, the melodies I'd tested quietly before school, the lines I'd rewritten again and again—they were more than childhood creativity. They were the beginnings of something real. Standing there with my award, I felt a sense of confirmation seep within me—not as pride, but as a truth that finally clicked into place.

Up until that moment, I had often wondered in quiet corners of my mind whether my passion was something I had imagined into significance or whether it truly held weight on a larger scale. Nashville answered that question for me. It told me that music wasn't simply a path that I loved—it was a path I was capable of walking with my own skill. And for the first time, I allowed myself to believe that my writing, my voice, and my perspective belonged not only in small-town rooms but in spaces that demanded excellence.

Winning didn't define me—but it surely refined me. It didn't make me feel superior; it made me feel aligned with my higher purpose. It grounded me in the belief that I wasn't chasing an illusion anymore. I was pursuing a calling. And Nashville, with its lights, sounds, expectations, and possibilities, had opened a door inside me that would never close again.

Hunger That Wouldn't Let Go

Nashville awakened my ambition like nothing else had before. Before that trip, I had passion, consistency, and a deep love for music that drove me to practice, write, and perform. But I hadn't yet developed the kind of focused, forward-moving ambition that pushes you beyond comfort zones. That changed the moment I stood among people who treated songwriting as a profession, not just a gift. Witnessing how much purpose filled the city and how seriously people approached their craft ignited something new in me. It wasn't just about wanting to write songs anymore. I wanted to grow. I tried to push myself. I wanted to see how I could take the talent I had and the discipline I was ready to build.

That ambition didn't come from comparison or competition—it came from alignment. Witnessing others live the life I'd only imagined showed me it was possible. Until then, I'd been counting stars in my imagination. Now, I had evidence. People were doing this—writing songs, performing, creating—and they were doing it with clarity, professionalism, and a clear sense of calling. I wanted to learn what they knew. I had the drive to walk with the same purpose. Nashville didn't change what I loved. It deepened my reason for loving it and gave it structure.

One of the most essential parts of that awakening was simply observing how industry professionals carried themselves. I watched their mannerisms, confidence, preparation, and presence. They weren't arrogant, but they moved with intention.

Everything about them seemed to say, "This is who I am. This is what I do."

That kind of ownership wasn't loud or flashy—it was steady. It showed in the way they tuned their instruments without hesitation, in how they spoke about their process with clarity, and in how they respected other musicians without feeling threatened. Their posture set the precedent long before their performances did.

I began to realize that artistry and professionalism weren't two separate identities; they were one that went hand in hand. The best musicians I encountered had both. They didn't treat creativity like a chaotic mystery; they treated it like a discipline. They showed up on time, honored their commitments, and made space for inspiration by building a strong structure around it. That balance between heart and skill fascinated me. I didn't want to just write songs that felt good—I wanted to develop the skills and mindset that would allow me to create consistently, share confidently, and work collaboratively. Watching the pros taught me that talent alone wasn't enough. Craft mattered. Effort mattered. Presence mattered.

Upon returning home, I did not have a trophy to signify a dream realized. Instead, I brought a new thirst for development. It was a restless, compelling energy that would not allow me to remain in my previous position. Nashville not only raised the standard but also turned the challenge into a competition. I never thought I had to demonstrate my abilities to anyone else—but I realized I had more to give, and now I wanted to see how much I was capable of. The place from where I had walked away surprisingly seemed smaller. Not because it lacked encouragement, but because I had grown in my perception. I had discovered more, so I wanted more, not in terms of material goods, but in terms of influence, quality, and relationships.

Every part of my routine shifted. I woke up to music on my mind—not just melodies, but goals, steps, and practice I needed to develop further. I began listening to songs differently—studying the lyrics, paying attention to phrasing, analyzing arrangements. I treated every track as a lesson. I wasn't just enjoying music anymore; I was learning from it. I treated every track as a lesson. What made this line stick? How did that chord change affect the emotion of the chorus? Why did one version of a song resonate more than another? These questions became part of how I thought and how I studied.

After that trip, I kept writing nonstop. Daily, occasionally even more than once a day, I would take my guitar and open my notebook. There was a point in me that had changed. I was no longer passive waiting for the muse to come. Instead, I was the one after it. I wouldn't care anymore if every line was excellent; instead, I would be concerned with the ideas just coming out. The inevitability of perfection became less intense. It was the forward movement that counted. The whole process was very dynamic, and even when I was not really happy with a song, I felt that writing it was helping me learn. My writing was now more like a stream, less like a struggle. I was taking risks, playing with rhythm and structure, and allowing the emotion to lead without over-editing before the idea could even breathe.

That season produced more songs than ever before. They weren't all polished or ready for performance, but they were real. They reflected growth. They showed me where I had been and pointed toward where I wanted to go. Every lyric felt like a step toward mastery. I was developing a voice—not just in tone, but in perspective. I became more open-hearted and started to work through my complicated feelings, seeking out and expressing truths I had never before considered. Nashville did not give me finished songs; it gave me the self-assurance to write the songs without any reservations.

I also began to experiment with lyrics in new ways. Prior to the trip, I just wrote down whatever came to mind first. But after the trip, I became more intentional in my writing, working on metaphors, double meanings, and even structure. I made it a point to write every song that could tell a whole story in just three minutes. I challenged myself to write songs that told a full story in three minutes. I tried writing from perspectives other than my own, crafting narratives that required empathy and imagination. I wrote in different keys, tried alternate tunings, and occasionally composed melodies before lyrics, rather than the other way around. I was exploring, not just expressing. And every single experiment was a lesson—about language, about feeling, about the intricate nature of expressing through music.

At times, I would stay up very late to write, with the guitar on my lap and half-finished lyrics on a torn piece of paper, and I'd stop and think: "This is it. This is what I want to do for the rest of my life."

That clarity didn't arrive with a single breakthrough— it was a gradual process, and repetition was its source of power. Every song that moved me to tears, every verse I rewrote five times, every melody that kept me up until sunrise added to the realization that music was not only my passion but also my identity.

There was no turning back. Once I had seen what was possible— once I had stood in Nashville, watched professionals live the life I longed for, and competed alongside them—I couldn't pretend music was just a side hobby anymore. It had always mattered to me, but now it demanded more from me. It asked for commitment. And I was ready to give it back.

Where Songs Became Symbols

After returning from Nashville, I didn't just write more—I wrote differently. I began experimenting with lyrics in new ways, exploring depth, structure, and emotion deliberately. Previously, songwriting had flowed mostly from instinct. I would pick up the guitar, hum whatever melody felt natural, and shape my lyrics around a raw feeling or passing thought. Something shifted after that trip. The process remained emotional, but it became more thoughtful. I wasn't just writing what I felt—I was shaping how that feeling was communicated, line by line, word by word.

I started paying closer attention to the mechanics of language, the way a single word could carry more emotional weight than an entire phrase. I rewrote more often—not out of doubt, but out of curiosity and confidence that I could go deeper. I tested alternate lines, refusing to settle for the first acceptable phrase, waiting instead for the one that landed with honesty and precision. I looked for clarity amid complexity, trimming excess, refining images, and trusting the silence between lyrics as much as the words themselves. This process didn't feel restrictive—it felt like growth.

Each revision became part of a dialogue with myself. The question I asked over and over was simple: "Is this what I really want to say?"

That trip made me pay attention not only to what I wrote, but also to why I wrote it. I wanted every line to carry purpose—even the most casual phrases needed to serve the story or hold emotional weight. I listened more closely to the songs I admired and realized that the ones that resonated most weren't always the most elaborate—they were the most truthful. I learned that truth didn't require grand vocabulary; it required courage and precision.

Nashville taught me that songwriting wasn't about showcasing skill—it was about surrendering to honesty.

Alongside this deeper approach to writing, I noticed another shift: my parents saw my determination intensify. They had always supported me, giving me room to explore music without force or pressure. But after Nashville, they saw a new level of commitment. I wasn't just "playing around" with music anymore. I was working on it, living in it, sacrificing for it. They watched me turn down social plans to stay home and write, heard the same song repeated late into the night, and noticed notebooks piling up, filled with crossed-out lines and unfinished verses. They saw that music wasn't just something I enjoyed—it was something I was choosing, again and again.

They didn't always understand the process, but they understood how deeply it mattered to me. My mom would peek into my room to make sure I'd eaten, only to find me still in the same spot hours later, guitar resting across my lap, paper balanced on my knee, absorbed, in a song I couldn't quite finish.

My dad would hear me humming down the hall and later say, "That one stuck with me."

Their quiet observations, their gentle questions, their willingness to listen as I shared my progress— those things offered support without expectation. Their belief never wavered, even as my writing grew more intricate and my ambitions stretched further.

What stood out most was how their encouragement evolved. They didn't dismiss my commitment as a passing phase; they treated it like a path. And in doing so, they permitted me to keep walking it. They didn't rush me or steer me elsewhere, as it's considered an unconventional path. Instead, they made space for the reality that music wasn't just something I did—it was the center of what I was building for myself. Their faith wasn't loud, but it grounded me in moments of doubt. Sometimes, all it took was a glance or a few steady words to remind me I wasn't creating in isolation. I was being seen, and that mattered.

As I continued to write and grow, my dreams began to outpace the boundaries of my small town. Streets that once felt expansive enough to hold my goals started to feel narrow—not because they lacked support or opportunity, but because my vision had grown. I started imagining stages I hadn't yet stood on, rooms full of strangers who knew my songs, studio sessions with people I hadn't met. These weren't fantasies—they were goals. Nashville had revealed what the music world looked like on a larger scale, and I couldn't ignore it. I didn't want to stay comfortable anymore; I wanted to break free.

I began researching songwriting retreats, contests, and co-writing opportunities outside my town. I looked for ways to connect with other musicians online, paying close attention to where people gathered to share their work and how they found their way there. My focus wasn't on fame—it was on forward momentum. I wanted to place myself in spaces that challenged me, spaces that demanded growth. The more I learned about the industry, the more strategic I became. I wasn't rushing, but I was deliberate. A clearer sense of direction guided each step.

Nashville became more than a memory—it became a symbol of possibility. It represented not just the trip I had taken, but the mindset I adopted because of it. Whenever I hit creative blocks or questioned my path, I pictured those music-filled streets, guitar cases clicking along the pavement, the sound of live bands spilling from every bar, the energy of creation humming in the air. That city had given me more than feedback—it had given me a sense of place. Even from miles away, I carried that feeling with me.

Sometimes, when I sat down to write, I imagined the room where I performed—the stage, the microphone, the audience. That moment, when my name was called as a finalist, it stayed with me. It wasn't about the prize. It was about being seen in a place that didn't owe me anything, being recognized in a city that demanded everything. That memory wasn't a reminder of success. It was a reminder of my divine alignment. When I thought of Nashville, I didn't think of competition. I thought of the clarity of my soul.

The clarity that comes when a private passion meets public recognition, when quiet effort is acknowledged by those who understand its value.

That clarity helped ground me when progress felt uneven. Not every song worked. Not every melody came easily. But I remembered what Nashville had revealed: the work matters. The practice, the revision, the discomfort of pushing through creative resistance— all of it had purpose. I wasn't writing for praise. I was writing because I had something to say, and I had learned that saying it well required time, courage, and discipline.

In the months that followed, I carried Nashville with me—not as a destination I had checked off a list, but as a reminder of what was possible in my life. It marked a turning point that reshaped my relationship with music. It taught me that songwriting could be more than expression. It could be a movement. It could become a legacy. And I was willing to give it everything I had.

From Spark To Lifelong Fire

Long before I understood the concept of "networking," Nashville taught me its value. I wasn't there with any business intentions, yet that's exactly what began to unfold in quiet, organic ways. From the moment I entered the competition to the final applause, I found myself meeting people who were just as passionate about music as I was. Some were fellow contestants; others were mentors, judges, or industry volunteers, all eager to support rising talent. Conversations sparked naturally—over lunch breaks, in line for registration, or while waiting backstage. These weren't formal introductions—they were genuine moments between people driven by the same creative spark.

Looking back, I realize that networking isn't about collecting contacts—it's about cultivating genuine connections with people who recognize your passion and see your true potential alike. One conversation about lyrics, a simple compliment exchanged after a performance—these moments planted seeds that would quietly grow. I discovered the power of surrounding yourself with people who not only speak your language but also challenge you to keep evolving in it. Nashville was my first encounter with a community that existed beyond geography. It showed me that music was more than personal—it was relational and revolutionary.

The relationships I formed during that trip weren't built on strategy or gain. They were rooted in authenticity. I spoke with others about songwriting struggles, shared drafts with others who offered constructive feedback, and encouraged those who, like me, were stepping into new and unfamiliar territory. In return, I was encouraged too. That mutual exchange—the back-and-forth flow of creative energy—was unlike anything I had experienced before. These weren't just fellow artists. They were mirrors reflecting my growth and reminding me of the areas where I still needed to stretch.

More than anything, I learned what it meant to support others without losing my own voice. In Nashville, collaboration wasn't competition. Artists weren't afraid to share what they knew best. I witnessed them recommending one another, introducing each other to new opportunities, and showing up to cheer on each other's performances. It was the opposite of cutthroat—it was about collective growth. Even as a newcomer, I was welcomed into that spirit. That experience reshaped how I viewed the concept of community. It made me want to be someone who could give as well as receive in my creative journey.

That experience also confirmed something for me on a deeper level: I could compete at higher levels. That may sound like a simple realization, but for someone coming from a small town, stepping into a space filled with seasoned artists, it carried real weight. Until then, I had only imagined what it would feel like to be taken seriously by people who truly understood the industry. Nashville replaced imagination with evidence. I didn't just hold my own in that competition—I earned a place in it. I didn't shrink under the weight of expectations—I rose to meet them. That shift in how I saw myself was transformative.

It's one thing to believe in your ability when surrounded by people who already love and support you. It's another thing to sustain that belief when no one knows your name and everyone around you is talented. Nashville showed me that I could stand confidently in that space—that I could contribute something meaningful to a space already full of creativity and still have a distinct voice. It was never about being the best there. It was about showing up prepared, genuine, and open to growth. That mindset is a foundation for how I approach opportunities moving forward.

Feeling both humbled and empowered at the same time was a paradox I hadn't expected, but it shaped me profoundly. I was humbled by the level of talent I witnessed—the commitment, the depth of experience, the polish of the performances. Many artists were far ahead of me on their journey, and I deeply respected that. But instead of letting that humility diminish me, I let it refine me. I didn't compare myself to feel smaller; I compared myself to learn. I absorbed everything—songs, feedback, small details— each one becoming a building block in my growth.

At the same time, I felt empowered.

Empowered because I was there.

Empowered because I had written something that earned its place.

Empowered because I didn't let the fear of being unproven stop me from stepping forward.

I didn't let uncertainty hold me in the back row. I walked into the room, sat among those who inspired, and delivered what I had to give. And that act alone shifted everything. It changed how I viewed not just my talent, but my resilience. I was stronger than I thought. More capable than I knew. And ready for more than I had imagined.

By the end of that trip, my love for songwriting was cemented in a way that would shape everything that followed. I had composed songs earlier, but Nashville taught me to write with a purpose. It wasn't about emotion alone—it was about craft. It wasn't about hoping someone would notice—it was about saying something worth listening to. I had already filled up my notebooks and taken part in family gatherings with my music, but this was a whole new experience. This was a song as a statement. A and B could not be any closer: I'm present, I have this feeling, and I want it to be known.

The moment of realization gave the process a new dimension in my respect. Songwriting stopped being something I did only when inspiration struck. It became a discipline. I began to consider it as a practice that required time, attention, and seriousness. I learned how to structure ideas, identify themes, and break through writer's block without waiting for the perfect mood. I realized that if I showed up consistently, the songs would be there too. They didn't always come out as refined or meaningful, but they came nonetheless. Gradually, those parts got transformed into whole pieces. Those whole pieces got transformed into performances. And those performances became the next steps.

Nashville was the spark that turned passion into a mission. Before that, I had always loved music. I knew it was a huge part of me. But after that trip, I knew it was the part of me that would define my whole life. Music wasn't just an outlet anymore—it was a calling. A place I returned to, over and over, not for comfort but for purpose. The city didn't just inspire me—it clarified me and opened me up to infinite possibilities. It helped me see that pursuing music wasn't indulgent or unrealistic. It was necessary. It was honest. It was work I was willing to do, even if it was difficult, even if it was slow, even if it required the sacrifice of time, money, and resources I had accumulated over the years of my practice.

And that shift—moving from interest to mission—transformed how I viewed life. Every choice, alteration of my schedule, and every minor decision regarding the allocation of my time started to be in sync with that mission. I wasn't just writing songs anymore. I was building something. A voice. A path. A legacy, however small it might have started. The spark that Nashville ignited in me did not extinguish; rather, it intensified. It still grows to this day. This is because once you visualize yourself in an environment that both challenges and encourages you, the change cannot be undone. You carry it with you— in your creativity, in your fearlessness, and in the notion that your truthfully narrated story is capable of connecting with others.

That's what Nashville gave me. Not just a moment of affirmation, but a direction for a lifetime. It gave me the kind of momentum that doesn't just push you forward—it keeps you awake. It keeps you honest. And most importantly, it keeps you going.

Chapter 4
The Song They Stole from Me

The Day The Music Turned Against Me

My mother's face told me something was wrong before she even spoke. It was a kind of look that simply freezes you—neither melodramatic nor overstated, but still so silent that it is heard louder than any shout. When she came into the room, she was standing there with the stiffest posture, probably trying not to let her feelings leak out. Her eyes, usually calm and warm, were unsettled. Her lips trembled slightly, though she tried to hide it. I was aware of the incident happening long before the words, and the doubt already formed a heavy burden in my stomach. My mother was someone who never got rattled easily, and her presence in this state of mind sparked a concern that made the room even cooler. Time seemed to stretch as she struggled to speak, searching for the right way to say something she didn't want to say.

When she finally found her voice, it came out soft and hesitant. She informed me that the previous day she had perhaps had an early-morning radio session—a common practice she often did while working around the house. But the tone in her voice now told me this wasn't a casual update about a new song she enjoyed. Again, she paused, as if announcing news that would weigh heavily. Then she said the words that shifted everything: she caught a song on the radio that was a real copy of one of mine. She took her time with the explanation. She outlined the tune, the arrangement, even the singer's emotional delivery. It was very obvious that every single detail was leading to the same conclusion. She was not confounded. She was not hypothesizing. She was definite.

As soon as she mentioned it, I felt like the air had been sucked out of the room. The speed of my heartbeat dropped so drastically that it seemed to me that it was hitting the floor. Hearing that my song—my creation, my expression—was on air, by the way, without me being aware of it, was like a sudden blow to my face. It wasn't the thrill of recognition; it was the shock of violation. I felt myself freeze as her words sank in. It was incomprehensible to me. I hadn't recorded that song professionally in a studio. I had not sung it in front of the audience. I hadn't given anyone permission to use it. The thought of it being somewhere, played and sung by another person, was beyond my imagination. My mother was looking me over cautiously, not knowing how I was going to take it, but my mind was already racing ahead, trying to make sense of what felt impossible.

As she continued describing what she heard, I realized at once which song she was pointing out. There was not even a speck of doubt. It was one of my most personal songs, and it had so much emotion associated with it that I had not shared it with many people. I had polished every line with utmost care, picking the words that would exactly convey the meaning I wanted. I could hear the melody in my head even as she spoke, remembering how I had shaped the chorus, the delicate pause before the bridge, the rise in the final verse. It was one of those things that could not be mistaken for any other song. It was of me. It contained my voice, my feelings, and my story. And even though she hadn't heard it often, she recognized its essence immediately.

A sinking dread accompanied instant recognition. The first thing I thought of was the envelopes I had sent out to various music companies months ago - hopeful submissions that had been sent with an optimism that was trembling. I remembered how excited, nervous, and eager I had been when I wrote those letters, believing that maybe, just maybe, someone would hear something in my music worth exploring. A sense of possibility had accompanied the sealing of each envelope. Could someone have taken the song? Could it have been copied? Could one of those submissions have fallen into the wrong hands? Just the thought made my stomach twist. I wanted to believe it was a misunderstanding, but the conviction in my mother's eyes said it wasn't confusion—it was stealing.

I acted quickly, driven by adrenaline and disbelief. I started contacting every company I had ever sent music to. My hands trembled as I went through old documents, gathering addresses, phone numbers, and contacts scribbled in margins. Each call felt urgent, every ring echoing the panic that was escalating inside me. When I couldn't reach anyone, I left voicemails, identifying myself, explaining what had happened, and why I was calling. Some numbers were outdated. Some companies had closed. Others transferred me from one person to another with no answers. Each failed attempt added to the growing fear that I was running out of options.

I continued to call regardless of the situation. I made up my mind that I wouldn't give up until I got a reply. The more calls I made, the heavier my anxiety became. I felt myself growing desperate, hoping someone would tell me it was a mistake.

I needed that person—any person—who was on the other end of the call to say, "We didn't use your song. You misheard."

But no one said anything like that. No one offered reassurance. I encountered nothing but silence, vague replies, or lengthy waits in place of the support I expected. My mother followed my movements in the room; with the phone glued to my ear, the emotions of fear and frustration grew stronger with every unanswered call.

Eventually, however, one record company—Columbine Records—gave a straight answer. As soon as I heard the company's name from the representative, anxiety gripped me. I had sent them the material months earlier. I remembered the submission clearly. I remembered the mixture of hope and hesitation I felt when I placed my envelope in the mailbox. Now, hearing their name again, I felt a strange sense of foreboding. The phone lady spoke in a neutral tone, but her message cut through with precision. She validated my darkest suspicion. They had indeed used a song that matched the details I described. They had released it under a different name, filed the documentation, and classified it as theirs.

The confirmation landed like a physical hit. For a moment, everything around me blurred. The room shrank, the air was thicker, and the sound of my heart became louder. Hearing those words from a stranger made the situation painfully real. This wasn't confusion. It wasn't a coincidence. It wasn't a mistake. It was theft. Someone, somewhere in that company, during the production process, took a part of my heart, an aspect of my identity, and claimed it as theirs. My mother watched my expression shift, confusion turning to shock, shock to devastation. She asked what they said, but I couldn't answer immediately. I had to contain myself.

The voice on the phone kept explaining, as it was an everyday business matter, all the way through. She listed the dates, the paperwork, and the recording information. She didn't hear the pain in my silence. It was a routine matter to her. To me, it felt like someone had reached into my chest and taken something irreplaceable. I was recalling every second of my life spent on that song—the unrefined feelings that I had conveyed through it, the sleepless nights that I had spent fine-tuning each line, and the quiet happiness that I had experienced when the tune was finally constructed into a piece. That song was not only a sound; it was a part of me. And now it was in the custody of someone else's name.

I remained motionless when the call ended. My mind was a chaotic place, with my thoughts circling and colliding with the unpleasant reality I was trying to avoid. Everything felt unreal and, at the same time, painfully clear. My mother sat beside me, trying to understand the depth of what had just happened. But this was more than a legal issue or a mistake. It was a violation of something sacred. My song had been snatched. My voice had been used unjustly. My trust had been broken by people I had never

even met. And in that moment, I felt something shift inside me—
a fissure that would alter the way I interacted with music for good.

The Weight Of What Was Taken

I really felt violated, a feeling that I had never undergone before,
since someone had snatched away a part of my soul. Moreover, it
was not just a single song. It was not just a piece of music with
lyrics and chords. It was a creation born from the deepest parts of
me, shaped by emotion, reflection, and vulnerability. Knowing
someone had taken it without permission, claimed it without
hesitation, and released it into the world as if it were theirs struck
at something far more personal than the notes on a page. It felt as
if someone took a diary, tore out a page, rewrote the name on top,
and acted as if the words were theirs. And the more I processed
what had happened, the more the betrayal grew, expanding inside
me until it reached every corner of my thoughts.

The first thing that came to my mind was disbelief. I kept going
over the whole situation in my head, trying to reason that it was
just a bad dream. My thoughts raced from hope to denial, looping
through questions that had no answers.

How could my song be on the radio?

Why would someone take it?

How did they think they could get away with it?

I desperately wanted to believe that there was indeed a mix-up;
maybe there was a similarity in the tunes, but it was not my song,
nevertheless. But the more I thought about it, the more I knew that
wasn't possible. I knew my own work. I knew the phrasing, the
tone, the emotional posture. Every part of that song held my
fingerprints.

Anger, powerful and consuming, was the second emotion I felt
after the disbelief vanished. It wasn't the explosive kind of anger
that shouts or breaks things. It was a deep, internal burn that sat

heavy in my chest. It stayed with me every moment of the day, a constant reminder of what had been done. I was not angry over my own actions. Not even the furious vocalist, who had at least carried my theme, pained me. No, it was the system that took an intimate thing away without being protected that drove me mad. I felt the unfairness press against my ribs, making it difficult to breathe. I wanted answers, accountability, justice—anything that could restore what I had lost. But there was no instant resolution. There was only anger, grief, confusion, and a profound sense of violation tangled together in a way I couldn't separate.

My parents, on the other hand, were determined to keep calm for me while I wrestled with my feelings. They saw the turmoil in my eyes, the way I walked around the house half-present, overwhelmed by the shock. They did not want to add to my pain by showing their anger or fear. Instead, they chose a firm and silent approach that, although my brain was in chaos, still managed to keep me rooted. My mother encouraged me to talk when I needed to and respected my silence when I didn't. My father stayed close, aware that sometimes presence speaks louder than words. Their calmness did not make my hurt disappear, but it provided support at a time when everything else seemed unsure.

However, I could feel their emotions under the skin of their calmness. My mother's worry showed in the way she kept watching me closely, as if trying to determine whether I was about to break. My father's jaw tightened when I spoke about what the representative had said. They were hurting too—not because they had lost the song, but because someone had stolen something meaningful from their daughter. They felt helpless in a way that parents rarely admit, forced to accept that some wounds couldn't be fixed with reassurance alone. Yet, they remained a constant and strong presence next to me, giving me a part of their strength at the time mine was weak.

Together, we decided to seek legal advice, hoping for justice. It felt like the only step that made sense, the only path that might give me back what had been taken. We gathered every document we had—copies of lyrics, mailing receipts, envelopes with dated stamps, and notes from my original drafts. We found a lawyer specializing in creative rights, someone who understood how vulnerable artists can be in a system that often values contracts over creativity. Sitting in her office, surrounded by papers that represented years of work, I felt both hopeful and terrified. Part of me believed that once she heard the whole story, she would find a path toward resolution. Another part feared that even with documentation, I might still lose.

When she reviewed everything, the professional mask covering her face melted away, replaced by a sadly kind one that sank my heart. She did not say anything for a long moment, but rather watched carefully every detail, turning the pages, looking at the dates on the envelopes, and comparing them with the registration documents we had obtained from the label. Each minute felt heavier than the last. Finally, she looked up and delivered the reality I had been afraid to hear. She told us that my "poor man's copyright," the sealed envelope I had mailed to myself in an attempt to protect my work, meant nothing legally. Courts didn't recognize it. Labels didn't honor it. It carried no weight in disputes, no authority in claims.

Hearing that crushed me in a way I wasn't prepared for. I had believed that the envelope offered at least some protection. I had thought that my effort to safeguard my work showed intent, originality, and authenticity. I had believed that hope mattered. But in the system's eyes, all those beliefs were irrelevant. Without an official, legally recognized, and adequately documented copyright registration, I had no claim. The song, according to the law, no longer belonged to me. It wasn't about morality, creativity, or truth. It was about paperwork I didn't have.

As the lawyer continued explaining the limitations of my situation, I felt myself shrinking into the chair. The feeling of powerlessness was like a heavy weight on me that I couldn't get rid of. I didn't understand why someone could walk away with my creation simply because they filed it first. I didn't understand why effort, originality, and honesty weren't enough. The law wasn't designed to protect the vulnerable—it was designed to protect the documented. And I hadn't known enough to protect myself. That thought was more painful than any other part of the experience.

I felt powerless in a system I didn't understand. I felt like a kid trying to find his way in a world where the adults not only understood but also enforced its rules. I felt lost, unseen, and profoundly discouraged. There was no path forward in that moment, no clear solution, and no obvious next step. Every question I put forth seemed to lead right back to the same point: there was nothing left for me to do. The injustice was real, but the options were nonexistent. My voice had been silenced, and the system offered me no way to get it back.

When we eventually exited the lawyer's office, I was protective of my documents, holding them tight to my chest as if I were trying to guard them against being taken away. But the song was already gone. The harm was done. And to my surprise, for the very first time, I doubted if I dared to go on. If a thing so intimate could be so easily taken away, what more could be robbed? If something so personal could be taken so easily, what else could be stolen? If the music industry were this merciless, was I prepared to keep on being a part of it? I had been through setbacks before, but this time it was different. This was my identity. This was trust. This was my voice being erased in real time.

Still, as the surprise turned into grief, a tiny fraction of me lingered on and didn't want the loss to be my definition. I didn't know how to move forward yet. I didn't know how to heal. But I knew I couldn't let someone else's theft be the final word on my story. This wound changed me, hardened me, and forced me into a new kind of awareness. However, even then, somewhere beneath the heaviness of all that I felt, a quieter truth had started to emerge.

I experienced pain, but I did not surrender to silence.

When Music No Longer Felt Safe

After leaving the lawyer's office, I felt like a foreigner in the very system I had once had faith in. I was officially powerless in a space I thought would welcome me. The world of music, which had always felt like home, was now viewed as a courtroom, with all the doors firmly locked. Everything I had worked for—the lyrics, the melody, the emotional truth I poured into that song—had vanished under the weight of technicalities and loopholes. My head understood the lawyer's explanation. My heart, however, refused to accept it. I was not legally entitled to anything, no copyright was registered in my name, and moreover, I had no means of restoring the loss. And because of that, someone else's name now rested over something that came from the deepest part of me.

The experience stripped me of more than just ownership. It also affected my self-esteem and shook the very base of my beliefs about the artistic process. I had grown up thinking that if I worked hard, stayed true to my voice, and created from a place of honesty, my work would be safe. But the truth I encountered was colder: talent meant little without protection, and the creative world could be just as cutthroat as any other. I hadn't been prepared for that. I hadn't been warned. No one had told me that sharing your work, even in pursuit of a dream, could make it vulnerable to people who did not care about its source. I felt like I'd been robbed in broad daylight, only to be told there was nothing I could do because the thief filed a report before I did.

This sense of powerlessness gnawed at me. I was carrying some invisible weight everywhere I went, feeling angry and exhausted at the same time. I couldn't sleep. I couldn't focus. I started to feel the loss every time I either picked up my guitar or opened my lyric notebook. Music no longer felt like a sanctuary. It felt like a battlefield. The very thing I had always turned to for peace and self-expression was now caught up with grief. Each note reminded me of what I'd lost. Each blank page felt riskier than before. I used to believe that creativity was a freedom. Now it felt like a liability.

Everything was in question: my objectives, my way of working, and even my career in music.

Could I still pursue this path?

Did I have the resolve to keep going, knowing how vulnerable I was without legal safeguards?

Could I bear the thought that it might happen again?

For the first time since I was a little girl, I wondered if my dream was too fragile for the real world. The heartbreak wasn't just emotional—it was existential. I wasn't just grieving a stolen song. I was grieving a belief I had carried my entire life: that authenticity would protect me. That integrity would carry me. That talent alone would open doors and keep me safe once I walked through them. I had to break free, once again, from scratch.

I had a hard time dealing with feelings of unworthiness. I started to internalize the theft as a reflection of my own failure.

I thought, Maybe I should have known better.

"Maybe I should have filed the proper forms. Maybe I wasn't smart enough to survive in this business."

This thinking led me down a dangerous path, one that clouded my judgment and made it hard to distinguish between what had been done to me and what I was afraid I had done wrong. I blamed myself for not being more prepared. I blamed myself for trusting. I blamed myself for being naive. It took time—and distance—to realize that the blame didn't belong with me. However, the shame felt as real as the loss during those first weeks.

And amidst all this, I made the effort to continue. I tried to write. I tried to sing. I tried to reconnect with the part of me that had always loved music without fear. But it was very challenging. My writing felt cautious. My melodies sounded muted. There was no joy in the process, only suspicion. I watched every lyric I wrote with wary eyes, afraid that releasing it into the world might lead to another loss. I didn't share my songs with anyone. I kept my songs to myself. I stopped going to open mics. I withdrew from every opportunity that used to bring thrills. Silence took the place of expression. Fear took the place of what I really lived for.

Still, there was something deeper I couldn't deny: I missed the part of me that music used to nourish. I missed the clarity, the emotional honesty, the sense of connection that came when a lyric fit perfectly or a chord struck the right nerve. I missed the way songwriting helped me process life—the good, the painful, and everything in between. I was aware that the total severance with music would mean the termination of my processing. And even though it felt dangerous now, even though it hurt, I couldn't turn my back on it entirely. Music was still my first language, the one I spoke best. And if I stopped speaking it, I feared I would lose something far more permanent than a single song.

One of the most difficult truths to comprehend was the fact that talent was not enough. No matter how pure your intent or how authentic your voice, the industry has rules. Some of those rules protect you—but only if you know them and follow them precisely, which, in my case, I failed to do. Others exist to maintain power and control. I was coming into this world with the idea that having a heart would be enough. But the whole experience taught me that a heart needs a protector. Talent needs structure. Creativity needs contracts. It's a lesson I wish I hadn't had to learn the hard way, but it shaped everything that followed. It changed the way I created, the way I shared, and the way I viewed success.

I learned to pay attention not only to inspiration but also to infrastructure. I realized that protecting your work is essential to valuing it. Just as you nurture a song into being, you also have to shield it once it's born. Copyrights, registrations, timelines, and documentation are all part of the process. I began researching, reading, and asking more questions. I no longer sent anything out without first understanding how it would be handled. I did not think that good intentions were enough anymore. I grew more alert, not due to any paranoia but purely as a matter of necessity.

However, it was still very hard not to be bitter. Some days, the bitterness was just under the surface, and it influenced every note

I played. Other days, it spilled out in tears I couldn't explain. I didn't want to be consumed by it, but it was there—raw and undeniable. I was angry at the person who stole from me. I was angry at the system that rewarded them. I was angry at how helpless I had felt. Yet the most important thing was that I was mad at how that single incident had affected my relationship with the thing I loved the most. Bitterness was my fight against that change. I didn't want music to become something I feared. I wanted it to be mine again—something pure, something healing, and something free.

I had to deal with the bitterness, so I wrestled with it. I neither denied nor hid it, but I also did not foster it. I let it rise when it needed to, acknowledged it, and then worked to move through it. I wrote about it—not in songs at first, but in journals, letters I never sent, long walks where I processed every feeling without needing to resolve it immediately. I had conversations with people I trusted, some were musicians, and others simply knew what it was like to lose something that cannot be replaced. Gradually and without being aware of it, I was healing.

Eventually, I returned to my guitar. Not with the same fire I once had, but with something quieter—a kind of reverence. I played the strings softly, as if meeting an old and quiet friend after a long time. The sound was familiar but carried a different weight now. Each chord was a reminder of what had been taken, but it was also a promise of what could still be done. I knew I wouldn't create carelessly again. I wouldn't share recklessly. But I also wouldn't stop. Because music, even in its most painful moments, still had something to offer me. And I still had something to offer through it.

That season of grief became a turning point. It was the dividing line between the artist I had been and the artist I was becoming. Before, I created with abandon. Now, I created with awareness. Before, I believed music would always protect me. Now, I realized I had to take care of my music as well. Yet, the song that was taken from me was no more; the lessons it left behind became the foundation for everything I would write from that point forward.

When Pain Became The Path To Purpose

Bitterness became my constant shadow since the theft of my song. It wasn't dramatic or loud—it lingered quietly beneath the surface, woven into moments that should have been joyful. Whenever I took my guitar in hand, even if it was just to play something totally different, that memory cropped up. I had to fight with it, and of course, I often had to fight with it more than once a day. It became a struggle to continue creating without letting that bitterness dictate the tone of everything I wrote. I didn't want to write angry music. I didn't want my voice, once rooted in hope and healing, to turn sharp and cynical. And so I made a decision, one that didn't come easily or quickly—I started doing the slow, conscious work of fighting bitterness, because I was not going to let it control me.

Letting go of bitterness didn't mean pretending it didn't exist.

It meant facing it and looking it in the eye.

To give it a name. To find out where it resided in me and what it had attached itself to.

I realized bitterness had formed around my fear—the fear that if one song could be stolen, maybe all of them could. That fear was the cause of the distance between me and my creativity. Breaking down that wall required acknowledging that music no longer felt safe. I grieved that loss more than anything. For years, music had been my refuge, the place I turned when everything else was uncertain. Now, it felt like a place of risk. My guitar wasn't a source of comfort for me like it used to be. It kept reminding me of what I had lost, what I could not keep safe.

Weeks went by without me ever touching it. One day, though, I was in my room and saw it from the other side of the floor. It appeared like a challenge to me—to take it and find out what was left.

Was the connection still there, or had it been severed?

I reached for it tentatively, my fingers brushing the strings without pressing them. The vibration of sound, soft and familiar, stirred something. Slowly, I began to strum—not the stolen song, but something new, something still forming. The notes were hesitant, like a language relearned after silence. However, as I was playing, it dawned on me that the music was still with me. It had just turned down the volume, waiting for me to come back without being scared.

I grieved that song—deeply, completely. It was not merely a matter of losing a set of lyrics and chords. It was about losing the trust that made creation feel safe. I let myself mourn that. I stopped trying to rush through the pain or hide it under false optimism. I sat with it. I wrote about it, not to publish, but to understand it. I remembered the day I wrote the song. I revisited the emotions that had inspired it. I honored the part of me that had once believed that sharing it would lead to opportunity, not loss. I cried when I pondered what had been taken from me, and there were more than one occasion to do so. But slowly, that grief transformed.

It was a moment of great agony, but it turned out to be very positive, as it changed my whole art practice in a lasting way. That moment, painful as it was, changed the way I approached my art forever. It taught me that creating comes with risks, but that creating anyway is an act of courage. I began writing again, first privately, then with more confidence. My notebooks filled up faster than they had in months. Besides, even though I still remembered what had happened, I had to make it not a ruler of my progress but a guide. Instead, I let it inform me. I protected my work. I documented everything. I learned how to register songs, track submissions, and navigate the business side of what I loved. The heartbreak became the reason I got stronger.

I didn't trust blindly anymore. I asked more questions. I read contracts. I learned from others who had experienced similar losses. There was a whole universe of artists who had gone through the same hardships before—artists who had to see their creations stolen, their names left out, and their voices used without recognition. They also reminded me that, though imperfect, this industry could still be navigated with integrity. I found mentors who taught me how to balance art and business, how to remain open without being naïve, and how to let my heart lead while keeping my eyes wide open.

Eventually, I stopped seeing the stolen song only as a wound. I started to think of it as a point of transformation. It was the cause that made me grow up—not as an artist, but as a person in the industry. It forced me to move from passion to purpose. Passion got me started. Purpose helped me stay. Purpose gave my writing a different depth, one born from lived experience. I no longer wrote just to express; I wrote to endure, to process, to guide others who might face the same kind of theft or heartbreak. I became more intentional, more focused, and more determined to protect the space I had fought to create.

And an unexpected thing occurred during that journey—I got my joy back. Not exactly in the same way I had felt it as a child, when everything was new and untouched. This joy was different. It was forged. Tempered. It had been tested, and because of that, it felt real. I no longer feared the process. I respected it. I didn't chase validation from outside sources. I chased alignment—between my voice and my values. I didn't try to prove myself to people who didn't respect the craft. I focused on building relationships with those who did.

The stolen song became a scar I carried with intention. It reminded me not of weakness, but of survival. It reminded me that I had something worth stealing—and that meant I had something worth guarding. I did not allow that scar to pull me back into silence. I let it remind me to keep growing. It taught me boundaries were not barriers. They were necessary lines of protection that allowed me to share my voice without fear. They allowed me to be generous without being vulnerable to exploitation. They allowed me to trust again—cautiously, but fully.

That one moment of theft became a symbol of resilience. Every time I wrote a new song after that, I knew what it meant to take that risk again

And every time I registered a new piece of work, I celebrated—not because it was a formality, but because it was a declaration:

This is mine. This came from me. This will be protected.

I stopped being afraid of the business side of music. I stopped seeing it as a distraction. I began to view it as stewardship—a responsibility to honor the gifts I had been given by treating them with care.

The music industry remained the same, with all its risks, pressures, and blind spots. But I had changed. I no longer approached it as someone hoping to be discovered. I approached it as someone who had already discovered her own worth. I did not long for the audience's approval to embrace me as a good artist; I was writing, performing, and creating because I was already very sure of who I was.

Now, when I look back on that moment—when my mother told me she heard my song on the radio—a feeling still rushes through me, but it's no longer bitterness. It's clarity. That moment showed me exactly what I was up against. It also showed me exactly who I was. And who I would become. It set ablaze the inner fire I was not aware I needed—the one that tempers character, endurance, and unshakeable trust in your own voice.

Yes, the song was indeed stolen from me.

But my story wasn't.

My voice wasn't.

My purpose wasn't.

That loss didn't bury me. It built me.

Chapter 5
Rebuilding Myself at Berklee

A New Chapter In A New Key

I attended college with the belief that knowledge would protect my gift. The sting of losing a song I'd poured my heart into taught me that raw emotion and faith weren't enough—if I had hope of safeguarding my creations, I had to do more. I had to get the training. I had to get the understanding. I had to learn the rules before I could trust the world with my voice again. When Berklee College of Music opened its doors to me, I felt I was being handed a second chance at life: a place where passion could be tempered with craft, and fledgling talent could be shaped into something resilient and lasting.

Arriving on campus was like stepping into a new universe—one built on music, filled with instruments, songbooks, and dreams in motion. The atmosphere was alive with opportunity. Around me, guitars slung over shoulders mingled with saxophones, keyboards, and sheet music; voices hummed in hallways; and everywhere I turned, I sensed the anticipation of creation. This universe was not like the quiet living room where I first got to know music, nor like the small talent shows I sometimes took part in. It was huge—a definite division between the "before" and "after" of my life.

In that first week, I quickly learned how much I had to unlearn—and the consequent relearning. On my own, I had relied on instinct, feeling chords by ear or chasing melodies by memory. But at Berklee, instinct alone didn't cut it. I was handed books filled with notation, shown how to read rhythm in fractions, and introduced to scales that stretched beyond familiar boundaries. I had to re-examine every comfortable chord, relearn proper finger positions, and understand harmony through theory instead of touch. The liberty that I previously cherished in music now appeared to be a strict, structured, and demanding set of rules—and part of me resisted. On the other hand, as I adapted, the value of those lessons became apparent. My old shortcuts gave way to precision, my guesses turned into understanding, and the raw edges of my playing began to smooth out.

Classical guitar was the hardest teacher of all. I had always played folk-style—easy chords, rhythmic strumming, melodies that felt natural to me. Classical guitar demanded something different: focus, discipline, and technique. Every finger placement mattered. Every rest, every pause, every plucked string required intention. I was required to learn to read music using the formal method, to decode notation, to synchronize with the metronome, and to master the control of dynamics with surgical precision. My hands trembled. My fingers ached. And the music at first sounded cold—too perfect, too composed, too detached from the raw emotion I associated with my songs. Yet behind the technical challenge, I discovered a new depth. I learned restraint, nuance, and subtlety. I realized that the most potent music often lives between the notes, in the quiet space where discipline and feeling meet. Classical guitar didn't erase who I was—it expanded what I could become.

Being surrounded by peers with talent and experience humbled me more than anything else. In dorm lounges or practice rooms, I'd hear someone working through complex jazz chords, another practicing scales with precision, yet another experimenting with percussion or vocal harmonies. I witnessed artists who were able to master varied techniques over the years, going into and even getting lost in classical training, or just exploring different genres I'd only heard of in passing. I felt small, unpolished, and raw. It would have been easy to shrink, to conclude I didn't belong. Instead, their talent reminded me of what it meant to be a student—someone always learning, constantly growing. Their focus, their discipline, their reverence for craft were louder than any clapping or praising. In such a company, humility was no longer a weakness but, rather, the very foundation of growth.

Humbled, yes—but not discouraged. Those first months of adjustment reshaped the way I thought about music. I slowly started to see it not only as a way of expressing one's feelings but also as a craft that needed to be developed, respected, and constantly mastered. I stopped playing by ear alone. I studied. I practiced scales. I learned sight-reading. I dissected chords. I experimented with melodies that challenged my old habits. I traced the lineage of songs, tried variations, and explored the technical underpinnings of harmony and rhythm. I spent hours alone with a classical guitar—fingers pressed firmly, eyes fixed on notation, hands striving for clarity. The calluses came through, but so did something else: confidence, not emotional but skill-based.

At night, I replayed old songs I had written before Berklee. With a new understanding, with new insight, I went back to the chord progressions, rewrote the bridges, and modified the harmonies. Some songs that once felt complete now sounded flat; others gained new life with subtle changes. It was strange and painful to see flaws, to admit that what I once believed to be enough had been limited. But there was also beauty in that realization. It meant growth. It meant evolution. It meant I wasn't the same person who wrote those lyrics in a small room. I was changing. I was building. I was refining.

This process didn't feel easy. Doubt crept in during long nights of practice. I questioned whether I was strong enough—if I had the discipline to sustain this. I wondered if the gap between where I started and where I wanted to go was too vast. I missed simplicity. I missed the ease of playing by feel. I missed the innocence of creating without structure.

Sometimes I looked at fellow students, marveling at their proficiency, and thought, "I don't belong here."

I questioned whether I was chasing a dream built on pain or creating a genuine craft. But each time I felt the doubt, I kept showing up. I practiced. I studied. I pushed a little harder. And slowly, as nerves became strength, hesitation became clarity, I felt myself transforming.

During my initial semesters at Berklee, I slowly connected together discipline and identity, training and voice. I started to see myself not just as someone who sings and strums but as a musician. As someone capable of reading, writing, and shaping music with intention. The stolen song—once a wound—became a driver. Its memory pushed me to demand more from myself: more knowledge, more skill, more understanding. I understood that if I ever wanted to get back into the music world with power, I would need a firm foundation that could endure heartbreak, deception, and doubt. Berklee was that stronghold.

My arrival on campus marked a turning point: a shift from innocence to preparation, from raw emotion to shaping, from uncertain hope to deliberate effort. I wasn't sure then what would come next.

Would I be the one to win or lose?

Would I get back what was gone or create something new?

One thing was for sure: I would no longer put my faith in talent or feeling alone.

I trusted discipline, learning, craft, and growth. I trusted my willingness to show up, to endure, to rebuild. And as I walked those hallways, carried a guitar case to class, sat in ensemble rehearsals, and studied notation under lamplight, I felt like I was reclaiming more than skill. I was reclaiming identity. I was redefining what it meant to be a musician and what it meant to belong to music—not just through songs, but through knowledge and integrity.

New Rhythms, New Bonds, New Identity

When I arrived at college and began classes, I quickly discovered that I was not alone in my passion—and that realization changed everything. I formed friendships that deepened my love for music, friendships I hadn't expected but came to rely on as much as I relied on my instrument. On the first day of ensemble theory, a fellow student with bright eyes and a well-worn guitar case introduced herself across the practice room.

She hummed through a chord progression I recognized, then smiled and asked, "Do you want to try that together?"

That simple invitation led to hours of shared practice, late-night songwriting sessions, and laughter over missed notes, and encouragement through frustrating stumbles. Together, we dissected songs, compared songwriting notebooks, and shared frustrations over lyrics that felt good in our heads but sounded flat when played aloud. Their presence expanded my world. I realized music wasn't just a solitary refuge for me anymore. It was a living, breathing community where voices blended—not just in harmony, but in hope. In their company, I rediscovered the joy of working together and the warmth of being in the same boat through difficulties.

This sense of community naturally merged with the academic rigor of formal music learning. I learned to read, write, and structure music more professionally than ever before. Theory classes introduced me to notation, rhythm parsing, chord progressions, and song frameworks. In sight reading drills, I learned to move beyond intuition and match notes with precision. In composition assignments, I discovered the structure of verse, chorus, bridge, modulation, dynamics, and tempo changes. The songs I once wrote by ear began to take on more precise shape on paper, with bars, measures, and time signatures guiding the flow. I practiced writing harmonic progressions in four-part harmony, experimenting with tension and release, dissonance and resolution—techniques I never considered when I simply followed my heart's impulse. The act of structuring music expanded my creative range. I realized passion was only the beginning; understanding form turned instincts into craft. My fingers, trained once to strum familiar chords, now navigated sheet music, read staves, and interpreted rhythms. My mind, once determined by feelings, became disciplined. This classical training did not take my spirit away; rather, it gave it a new voice.

My choir experience was a contributing factor to my growth. Joining the college choir introduced me to a style of discipline and teamwork that portraits of solo performance rarely show. Instead of holding a guitar, I sat in a row of chairs among dozens of voices, each person's part weaving into a larger tapestry. Choir practices meant being on time; that is, arriving early, warming up, tuning, and blending, doing everything together. Learning to match pitch, stay in key, and listen—really listen—to surrounding voices taught me humility. Sometimes one voice soared; sometimes one voice faltered; the strength of the song depended not on solo brilliance but on collective coherence. Breath control practices, timing exercises, vowel uniformity, and synchronized dynamics shaped a new musical muscle: awareness of others. I learned that performance wasn't always about standing out—often, it was about contributing to something bigger. Choir deepened my appreciation for harmony, not just in music but in unity, reminding me that every individual voice matters but only when blended with respect for the whole. The lessons I learned there carried over into songwriting, rehearsals, and collaborations. I started thinking less about "my song" and more about "our sound," and about how music can connect people rather than just express feelings.

Summers brought a different kind of growth: from academic structure to real-world fluidity. During the summer breaks, I went on tour with bands – a transition from huddled classrooms and concert halls to open-air stages, small-town gigs, backrooms, and road traveling. Those summers with touring bands expanded my musical flexibility in ways I couldn't have predicted. I played with diverse musicians—drummers, keyboardists, bassists, horn players—each with their own style, rhythm, and background. One summer, I was a jazz-influenced backup singer; another, I was playing acoustic for folk-inspired ballads; yet another, I was part of rock arrangements under flashing lights and noisy crowds. Switching genres meant adapting not only my voice and technique, but my mindset. I learned to listen for subtle tempo changes behind drum beats, to find space in busy horn arrangements, to match volume with electric instruments, and to hold my ground when songs shifted on the fly. I carried notebooks filled with chord charts, set lists, and performance notes. I learned to respond dynamically—not just play what was written, but anticipate shifts, support others, and improvise when needed. Touring not only broadened my skill set but also gave me greater self-assurance. I came to realize that my musical identity could be as big as one genre, one style, or one comfort zone.

Moreover, I stumbled upon unfamiliar genres that were not on my prior experience list. I came through a gateway of jazz, classical crossover (especially the kind that is very much like and mixed with world music), soul, and R&B— the same as R&B—these were the styles I had only previously admired from a distance but never dared to come close to. In one late-night dorm discussion, a roommate played an Afrobeat track that sent syncopated rhythms pulsing through the room. Another friend introduced me to a flamenco inspired guitar progression. In class, we studied modal scales and experimented with Latin rhythms. My guitar morphed—no longer just a comfortable folk companion, but a versatile instrument capable of carrying complexity, nuance, groove, and soul. I spent hours learning unfamiliar chord shapes, exploring rhythm patterns, practicing muted strums, syncopation, and arpeggios. I tried singing over jazz standards, feeling the melodies dance in ways I'd never known. Each new genre felt like a doorway, a soil in which I could plant new seeds of sound. And with every step, I realized that my definition of "what kind of musician I was" was broadening. I was no longer just a folk song girl from a small town. I was a student of music—open, flexible, evolving.

Despite this creative expansion, uncertainty often returned. I struggled with uncertainty, especially on lonely nights when the weight of expectations and new challenges pressed down. I asked myself whether the serious musicians' world was meant for me, whether I could be as disciplined as they were, and whether the one song I had taken—the one so full of fear and vulnerability—would always be there to haunt me. But I kept showing up. I practiced scales even when theory made my head spin. I went to choir practice even when it seemed impossible to blend the different voices. I toured summers despite fatigue and homesickness. Instead of giving in to fear, I showed up again and again. Every time I faced difficulty—a wrong chord, a missed note, a shaky harmony—I leaned into the challenge rather than away. I let mistakes guide me rather than paralyze me. And slowly, over time, those moments of insecurity became milestones in my growth.

Boston became more than a city for education—it became a chapter of growth and independence. Living in dorms, managing schedules, balancing classwork with practice, and building friendships abroad while adhering to my hometown norms, I matured outside music as well as within it. I learned to budget time and money, to stagger study sessions, to snack at odd hours between rehearsals and schoolwork. I discovered the meaning of accountability: if I missed class or skipped practice, I wasn't just letting myself down—I was affecting a whole ensemble. I had to watch the due dates for theory essays, ear-training assignments, composition submissions, and, at the same time, performance. I went through stress, the occasional burnout, and homesickness. But I also learned resilience, time management, and self-care. The framework of college life required discipline not only in music but in everything else as well. And I took those lessons with me everywhere I went.

Through all of this, I felt myself maturing both musically and emotionally. I wasn't the naive girl who believed writing songs was enough. I was turning into an artist with a good deal of knowledge, technique, flexibility, and, above all, maturity. I analyzed why certain chord progressions stirred emotion. I considered how arrangements affected a song's impact. I listened differently. I felt more deeply. I cared not just about lyrics, but about structure, arrangement, performance nuance, and emotional truth. My identity shifted: I was no longer just a singer-songwriter chasing dreams, I was a musician in the making, learning to balance heart and skill, feeling and discipline, vulnerability and professionalism. That balance began to shape everything I wrote, every note I played, and every relationship I built.

Behind the scenes of growth, the memory of the stolen song still haunted me—but less as a wound, more as fuel. Every time I learned a new scale, every time I mastered sight reading, every time I blended vocals in choir, I felt I was reclaiming power. I promised myself that I would never again allow the guardrails to be absent in my creative journey. I became vigilant about protecting my work, documenting it, safeguarding it, and understanding the business side of music. The theft taught me the harsh truth, but Berklee taught me the tools to survive it. My fear that someone could just take my creative output without accountability was gone. Instead, I was learning to carry not only a guitar but also the burden of responsibility.

My time in college strengthened me for the opportunities ahead. It transformed pain into purpose, insecurity into structure, raw passion into informed artistry. It didn't erase the past—it reshaped it. And as I walked out of dorm buildings into Boston's autumn air, guitar case in hand, I didn't just carry a handful of songs. I brought a new identity: one forged in loss, tempered by education, shaped by community, and ready to face whatever stage lay ahead.

Doubt, Discipline, And Becoming

A cloud of uncertainty loomed over me like a limb during the first few months in college. I often wondered if I belonged among classmates whose fingers danced effortlessly across strings and keys, whose voices carried with apparent ease even under pressure.

So, whenever I entered the practice room or opened the workbook for theory, the whisper was back again: Maybe you don't have what it takes.

It wasn't dramatic—just a quiet questioning voice buried beneath ambition and hope. I could feel it when I had problems with a new chord progression or when I went through a sight-reading exercise quite clumsily, and it would tighten my chest. Doubt threatened to freeze every attempt before it even began.

But I kept coming back. I forced proud feet into unforgiving practice rooms. I refused to let that whisper win. Day by day, after class, after completion of homework, I went back again and again to my guitar or piano—whatever instrument needed my attention the most. I repeated scales until my fingertips called for mercy. I opened sheet music under lamplight late into the night. I took part in all the choir rehearsals, ensemble sessions, and workshops that I could find, even when the luxury of having strength was gone. I handed in theory papers before the deadline, even when my mind felt muddled and weary. I showed up not because it felt easy, but because I believed faith without effort was fragile. And with each session I survived, I chipped away at doubt, brick by stumbling brick.

Living in Boston, Massachusetts, during those years transformed me in subtle but profound ways. I learned to navigate more than musical theory—I knew life. Dorm kitchens, tight schedules, balancing meals with practice, budgeting time like currency—all became part of the daily rhythm. I woke before dawn to catch buses to campus. I juggled academic assignments, rehearsals, and late-night writing sessions. I cooked meals between classes, studied harmony in cafés beneath autumn skies, and warmed my hands with coffee after winter walks home from class. I discovered the kind of independence that demands responsibility, and in that independence, I found a new version of myself—one capable of survival, growth, and self-reliance.

The coexistence of strict study and creative writing became a daily balancing ritual. Theory classes demanded precision—sight reading, rhythm drills, composition homework, harmonic analysis. Choir sessions called for blend, discipline, and responsiveness to others. Ensemble rehearsals tested timing, coordination, and adaptability. Then there were composition projects and songwriting assignments—spaces where creativity was rewarded, but expectations were high. I learned to treat music not as spontaneous emotion, but as a disciplined craft. I built schedules that prioritized practice and homework, structure and spontaneity. I discovered that the best creative breakthroughs often came after discipline was already in place—after finger calluses, after repeated correction, after the hard work of mastery. The balance was indeed sensitive, yet every time I succeeded in maintaining it, I felt more grounded and more competent.

Back then, musically and emotionally, I did not recognize the pressures I was facing. My reflection on the past now reveals my transformation: I wasn't the girl who played in living rooms anymore. I was becoming a musician who could read, write, interpret, collaborate—someone who understood that voice and vulnerability were precious, but so were practice and precision. I began writing songs not only from heartbreak or hope, but from observation, insight, and experience. I was layering instrumentation, playing with the loudness, and finding the quietness in the pauses between notes. And with every piece I composed, I was convinced more and more that music was not just a hobby for me—it was the person I was becoming.

Competition, which at one time was a remote concept from childhood talent contests, was now presenting itself in a novel way—recitals, ensemble auditions, theory challenges, and peer critiques. At first, I approached them with hesitation. Comparison was dangerous. However, little by little, I was employing rivalry as an instrument—not to show that I was the best, but to perfect my skill, to stretch my limits, to go beyond the barriers. Instead of envy, I felt motivation. I asked questions. I observed techniques. I practiced harder. Whenever I performed in duet recitals, choir concerts, or late-night gigs, I approached it with seriousness. I wasn't chasing applause. I was chasing growth. Every performance, whether polished or flawed, became feedback—a signpost on the path to becoming stronger, more intentional, more professional.

This approach shifted something inside me: success no longer looked like validation or praise—it looked like improvement—a clean chord transition. Accurate timing. A harmony held without wavering. A lyric that resonated. A polished performance free of shaking hands or a cracking voice. These little victories were more significant than any diploma. They were evidence that effort, structure, and perseverance could rebuild what had been wounded. They demonstrated that I was no longer dependent on the past or in fear—I was able to progress. I could create something new, grounded not just in emotion, but in craft.

Between classes, practice sessions, and performances, life outside music shaped me too. The streets, seasons, and solitude of Boston were all part of my development. I learned how to drag my guitar case through the snow-covered sidewalks, to do ear training by candlelight in the dormitory rooms, and to compose lyrics based on the flickers of the city and deep-night talks with global friends. I discovered resilience not only in skill, but in adaptability. I managed finances, time, relationships, responsibilities, and creative ambitions—often all at once. And that juggling strengthened me. It taught me endurance. It taught me discipline beyond the strings and staves. It taught me life harmonized with music.

It was an emotional process for me to learn how to detach my identity from my output. The stolen song once defined me—pain, loss, betrayal seemed part of my creative signature. But through struggle and growth, I realized that who I was didn't depend on a single composition. My identity was broader: a student, a collaborator, a musician building with integrity. Then I started viewing music as a continuous, developing trip instead of a delicate dream. I wrote songs that didn't merely express heartbreak, but told stories, explored hope, and invited empathy. I found confidence not in perfection, but in persistence. I held tight to the belief that growth mattered more than speed, that learning mattered more than applause.

Nonetheless, there were still the nights when uncertainty would sneak back in. I would stare at sheet music, pencils poised, and wonder if I would ever match the talent I admired. I wondered if my voice, shaped by loss and longing, would ever find full strength. I doubted the music business—a large, unpredictable world— But each time I felt that doubt, I returned to practice. I returned to theory. I returned to writing, chords, melodies, and harmonies. Because if music had taught me anything, it was this: healing comes not from avoiding pain, but from continuing through it, reshaping it, growing because of it.

At the end of those college years, I was a changed person. Not just older, not just more experienced, but transformed. Gone were the days when I was merely a small-town singer-songwriter who had lost his way. I was a musician with training, resilience, and purpose. My hands could read notation. My heart could write truth. My mind could be structured. My spirit could persevere. I didn't know where the future would lead—but I knew I was ready. Tools in hand, scars acknowledged, voice intact, I faced the road ahead with something more substantial than hope: readiness.

In retrospect, I realize that Part 3 of my story was not just about surviving college. It was about rebuilding from the inside out— rebuilding trust in my music, confidence in myself, and trust in the process. I learned that discipline doesn't dampen passion—it protects it. I realized that independence doesn't isolate—it empowers. I learned that growth isn't always visible, but always real. And I got to know that even when doubt and loss come up as enemies trying to silence a voice, if one chooses to keep on showing up, that can plot a new future.

I came out not just healed but also stronger. Not only skilled, but grounded. Not just hopeful, but equipped. I remained me—with scars, stories, and a song stolen—yet I was remade. And through that remaking, I discovered not just the music but also the perseverance; not only the tune but also the grown-up; not only the desire but the self.

From Student Roots To Wings—How College Reshaped My Music And My Mission

College taught me that collaboration is more than sharing notes or voices—it is the very lifeblood of music's potential. In ensemble rehearsals, songwriting workshops, and impromptu jam sessions in dorm lounges, I discovered that a melody meant for one becomes stronger the moment other instruments, voices, or perspectives join it. I still recall one night, I took a simple guitar sketch to a composition class. The solo piece seemed sincere but dull to me—not yet tried by life. A classmate suggested a cello line to support the vocal melody. Another offered a subtle harmony in the chorus. Hesitant yet hopeful, I agreed. When those parts came together, the song breathed, stretched, and transformed. Harmony enriched emotion. Resonance added dimension. What was once fragile became layered, rich, and alive. That moment taught me that music seldom flourishes alone. It thrives when hearts, instruments, and intention unite. Collaboration didn't dilute my vision—it expanded it. That lesson stayed with me, shaping the way I approached every composition, every performance, and every creative partnership.

Alongside collaboration, college revealed a truth I hadn't fully grasped before: raw talent without structure is like a riverbed without banks—capable of flowing, but easily scattered. At Berklee College of Music, that instinct and feeling were no longer exclusive but still quite powerful. Scales practiced with precision, endless sight-reading drills, harmonic analysis, rhythmic discipline—these became tools, not chores. I traded carefree strumming and intuitive chord changes for metronome counts, notated arrangements, and rigorous rehearsal schedules. I practiced muscle memory until my fingers remembered patterns before my mind did. I analyzed songs not just by sound, but by structure: how chords resolved, where silence energized, how dynamics carried emotion. I altered arrangements to make transitions tighter, to smooth the syncopation, and to draw out the release and overwhelm the tension. With every corrected mistake and polished measure, I felt the foundation under my music strengthen. Structure became a scaffold, not a cage. It enabled creativity to soar safely—with clarity, intention, and durability. I discovered that it is passion that sets the fire, but it is discipline that keeps it burning.

My technical abilities developed, and my cooperative activities grew more intense, so I slowly began to identify with a different persona—not a singer hanging on to lyrics and melody, but a musician of depth, awareness, and versatility. The shift came quietly. Overnight, I stopped thinking only about voice and guitar. I started thinking in layers: melody, rhythm, harmony, counterpoint, texture, and instrumentation. I experimented with fingerstyle, classical guitar techniques, and light percussion—not to imitate others, but to expand my vocabulary. In ensemble rehearsals, I listened first. I learned to blend, to support, to adapt, rather than to dominate. I practiced translating the emotional core of a song into orchestration, subtle harmonies, and arrangement choices that honored integrity over flash. I played in jazz combos, classical guitar trios, and vocal ensembles—each context teaching me a different facet of musicianship. The identity inside me grew. I have not only been a singer-songwriter but also a composer, arranger, collaborator, and all-encompassing musician. That identity altered my dreams, my expectations, and my creative morals.

As I became more musically powerful, the stolen song memory remained, a soft echo in the background of my mind. It would come and go at times; for instance, when I was tuning my guitar before going to bed or while opening a new lyrics notebook, waiting for the breath of inspiration. The betrayal felt like a scar—raw, sensitive, and unavoidable. For a long time, I carried shame and grief wrapped in fear. But during my college years, something changed. I began to transform that haunting into fuel. I made a decision: every new song I wrote would be treated with awareness, respect, and protection. I meticulously documented drafts, archived dated recordings, kept notes on all collaborations, and registered compositions whenever I could. I understood that creativity without boundaries—without respect for rights, for origin, for clarity—was vulnerable. So, I refused to be naive. I became vigilant. I would not see music merely as an expression but also as a property—a property that needs to be taken care of, managed, and honored. The theft did not define me. It became a sign and a push.

This resolve didn't just shape how I protected my work—it shaped how I shared it. I approached collaborations differently. Before handing over a lyric or melody, I clarified roles, asked questions, and insisted on mutual understanding. The only people I trusted were those to whom I sent demos. I documented rehearsals, credits, and dates. I highlighted every version, every change, and every contribution. I demanded respect, transparency, and agreement. Some people turned down the offer, and some just left. But those who remained were the true collaborators who appreciated the art, not the advantage. Through caution wrapped in commitment, I reclaimed my voice. I rebuilt trust—not in naïve optimism, but in intentional creation. That vigilance became part of my musical identity. I learned that integrity matters more than exposure. That a protected creation can reach further, last longer, and honor both artist and audience.

As graduation approached, I felt the transformation solidify. I no longer walked into the final recital with dreams of approval or sudden success. I walked in with tools. I had technique, theory, practice, awareness, accountability, and community. I had experienced heartbreak and betrayal—and I had healed, learned, and rebuilt. I didn't get up as a naive, idealistic person, but as a musician ready. My hands were skilled, my brain was disciplined, my feelings were protected, and my sight was focused. I had overcome the fear of being exposed. I came to making art with caution and reverence, not with a wild and reckless attitude. I understood that music demands more than emotion. It requires commitment, consistency, and character.

When I crossed the stage to receive my diploma, it didn't feel like a conclusion. It felt like the laying of a foundation—a firm base from which to build everything that came next. I carried with me more than a string of credits. I put in hours of practice, notes, charts, recordings, collaborations, contracts, and, most importantly, renewed trust in my voice. I left college not just with lessons learned, but with a purpose defined: to create with heart, to protect with integrity, to build with discipline. A vast, unpredictable, and uncertain world had found a counterpart in the steadiness of my readiness.

When I reflect on that chapter, it seems to be a continuous rebirth. The stolen song is no longer in the limelight for my character. It is a blaze that fused delicacy into iron. The ache is no longer an obstruction to my speaking. It pushes me to refine. The fear no longer paralyzes me. It grounds me in preparedness. Through late-night rehearsals, solo practices, collaborative efforts, registrations, and structural studies, I rebuilt not just my songs—I rebuilt my identity. I moved from youth's hopeful uncertainty into maturity rooted in knowledge, respect, skill, and community.

I don't write music the way I did when I was nine or even when I first entered college.

I write with intention.

I write with awareness.

I treat every rhyme, every chord, every melody, and every collaboration as sacred.

I protect what I create.

I honor those who create with me.

I guard against silence that hides theft.

I step into studios, rehearsal rooms, creative spaces, not with naive trust, but disciplined readiness.

I have learned that music is more than sound.

It is a craft.

It is a connection.

It is accountability.

It is a promise—to self, to collaborators, to audiences.

My college experience did not assure my success. Nevertheless, it provided me with the integrity to create, the resilience to endure, and the conviction to build music that lasts not only for today but for all the tomorrows I will write—something far more significant.

And so, I walk forward, guitar case in hand, heart steady, spirit renewed, not as someone chasing fleeting applause but as a person devoted to the lengthy path— aware, prepared, grounded, alive.

Chapter 6
The Contest That Changed Everything

The Invitation I Didn't Expect

I still remember the exact moment I heard it—that brief, almost forgettable announcement on the radio that felt like it was meant just for me. It arrived at an unremarkable afternoon's peak, tucked between promotional jingles and a very soft piece of music that I had hardly noticed. My attention wasn't even focused on the show. The radio was just on, filling the silence of my drive with static and sound.

Then came the words: "Calling all aspiring songwriters—submit your original song for a chance to be heard on the national stage. Deadline approaching. Details online."

I froze. My grip on the steering wheel tightened instinctively. I couldn't explain it, but something deep inside me shifted in that moment—like a sudden beam of light piercing through months of gray. I experienced a sudden shock, was left breathless, and felt as if destiny had just spoken in my ear. The whole series of events, including the block, the theft of my song, and the void inside me that had been there all along—this moment seemed to be like nothing else. It was as if life had finally thrown me a lifebuoy.

I don't usually believe in signs. But that day, I did. The announcement, though brief and informal, seemed preordained. I had the impression that some power had seen my suffering and had decided to offer me a fresh start. Not to erase the past—nothing could do that—but to reclaim something I thought had been taken from me forever. The stolen song had left a wound I hadn't figured out how to close. But this contest... this was a possibility, and it felt personal.

Returning to campus later that day, everything looked the same—the red brick buildings, the winding sidewalks, the buzzing energy of students rushing to and from classes—but something had changed in me. I moved through familiar spaces with an unfamiliar purpose. The heavy fog that had clouded my days slowly began to lift. Clarity and even excitement were feelings that I experienced for the first time in months. It wasn't that I was just returning to my regular pace; it was like I was bringing something with me—hope.

I was familiar with the practice of keeping my head down. The episode involving my lyrics being stolen had reduced my social interaction in ways that I hadn't even noticed at the start. Music had become a sore subject, and songwriting—once my joy—became something I avoided. I tried to redirect my focus, bury myself in academic routines, and act as if none of it had affected me. But it had. And now, with this contest in front of me, I realized just how much. Cause I wanted to care once more. I wanted to take the risk, even though it scared me.

That night, I sat down to fill out the application. Opening the laptop and bringing up the contest form was a shaky process for my hands. The questions were easy. Name. School. Contact information. Title of the song. Type of music. However, I had the impression that I was dealing with something more important than filling a form. Each keystroke felt heavy. Emotional. Sacred, even. Because I wasn't just applying to a contest—I was stepping back into something I thought I had lost the right to. I was permitting myself to believe again.

The title of my song—which I had written during one of the hardest times of my life—was typed by me, and I was looking at it on the screen. It was very strange to see it like that. That song had been silent for a long time, covered by disappointment and doubt. Now it was getting up again.

Then I got to the question that caused me to come to an abrupt stop: "Who will perform your song?"

I stared at the screen. The keyboard was under my fingers, but they stayed still. My mind wasn't ready for that next step. Composing the tune was easy. Then, picking a person to perform it—a person to give the words life—was hard. I hadn't realized how exposing that decision would be.

This song wasn't just music. It was my story, my sorrow, my hope, all tangled into melody and verse. To pass it on to someone else was to put whole trust in them regarding a very personal matter. I never experienced the creation of music with anyone else before— definitely not a piece that was so near to my heart.

My mind ran through a mental list of possible names—people I knew who could sing. But none of them felt right. I didn't just need a voice. I needed the voice. A person who would not only perform the song but would also feel it, connect with it, and honor it—someone who would be able to bear its emotional burden without even attempting to make it sparkle.

I had nearly closed the form. I felt, as it were, paralyzed in fear and inspiration, so that so many awkward things all meshed together.

What if I chose the wrong person?

What if I submitted the song and it got ignored—or worse, mishandled again?

That's when a few friends, who had wandered into the lounge where I sat filling out the form, noticed what I was doing. I explained the contest—briefly, cautiously—and mentioned that I didn't know who should sing the song.

They looked at each other, then one of them said, "You should ask Debbie."

I blinked. "Debbie?"

"Yeah, you know—Debbie Mitchell? She's pre-med. Quiet. But she sings like you wouldn't believe."

It was clear to me who they were referring to. Debbie was a constant figure on the campus—once in the library, the science building, the cafeteria—but there was only a tacit nod between us. She was always solitary, either totally engrossed in her books or hurrying to the labs. Singing was something I had never resonated with her.

The suggestion felt random at first. Still, with each passing moment of deep reflection, the level of my intrigue grew ever higher. Debbie was not the type of person who would be in the center of attention, and hence did not have the spotlight energy of someone looking to be the center of attention. To me, she was down-to-earth, serious, and indeed very thoughtful. And if what my friends said was true about her voice, maybe she was precisely the kind of person I needed—someone who could sing with soul, not ego.

Still, the idea of approaching her filled me with nervous energy. I didn't know her. We had no history. There was no way for me to know what her answer was going to be. Moreover, to tell a person to sing this song—a song which meant so much to me—was like giving them a delicate part of me.

But something in me knew I had to try. Maybe this was the next step in the journey fate had started when I heard that radio announcement. Perhaps the contest wasn't just about reclaiming my music. Maybe it was about learning to trust again.

So, I made the decision. I would approach Debbie. I would explain the contest, share the lyrics, and ask if she'd consider singing it. It would be a leap of faith, no doubt—but one that felt necessary. At the bottom of my heart, I was sure that this was not simply a matter of having my music listened to. It was about getting better.

And getting better, I came to realize, is one of the things that often starts with the brave step of inviting someone to be with you. No matter how little you might know each other.

No matter if the response is a no.

Even if it scares you.

Finding Her Voice, And Trusting Mine

The decision to approach Debbie wasn't just about asking someone to sing. It felt bigger than that—like stepping into unfamiliar territory, with no guarantees. She and I had no real relationship. We'd passed each other in campus halls, maybe exchanged a few courteous nods in the dining hall, but beyond that, she was a stranger. And yet, in that moment, I believed she might be the right person to bring my song to life. However, this belief did not help me at all to take that walk across the campus to the spot where she usually was—head buried in a medical textbook, earbuds in, lost in her own world.

Approaching her felt like a leap of faith. It was not that I feared she would laugh or outright reject me, but rather that it would be giving a piece of my heart to a person I was not at all sure of. This song was not merely a tune I had put together, but instead was born out of a period of sorrow, introspection, and uplifting. To hand it over was to invite someone into that personal space, and I didn't know how she would treat it.

Still, I found her one afternoon near the biology building, seated at a quiet outdoor table with her notes spread out. I walked up, heart pounding, rehearsing my words in my head.

"Hi, Debbie, you don't really know me, but…"

No version of that opener felt right. But there's never a perfect time to risk vulnerability, only the moment when you choose to do it. So I did.

She looked up, a little surprised to see me standing there. I introduced myself, reminded her of the mutual friends who had suggested her name, and then, without over-explaining, I told her about the contest. I said I'd written a song and needed a vocalist. I have been looking for somebody who could bring more than just technique, and instead bring a feel for the spirit behind the lyrics.

She fell silent for a while. She just stared, her expression unreadable. I braced for an awkward decline. But then, without hesitation, she said, "I'd love to."

Just like that.

I blinked, unsure if I'd heard correctly. Her voice was calm but genuine. Not overly excited, not theatrical—just solid, confident, open. I didn't realize how tightly I'd been holding my breath until that moment.

"You would?" I asked, the disbelief probably showing on my face.

She smiled. "Sure. I love singing, and I've always wanted to work on an original song. If you think I'm the right fit, I'm in."

It felt like something inside me exhaled for the first time in weeks. It was not just agreement; she responded with a quiet enthusiasm that convinced me I'd made the right decision.

We agreed to meet the following evening in one of the campus music practice rooms. It wasn't a glamorous spot—just an old room with soundproof walls, a slightly out-of-tune upright piano, and poor fluorescent lighting. But it didn't matter. It was private, quiet, and just what we needed.

When she arrived, Debbie brought a small notebook, a water bottle, and her curiosity. I got my guitar and a copy of the lyrics, printed neatly on a single page. The atmosphere was quite odd—less so, but still electrified. It was the kind of tension that arises when two individuals get involved in something new and significant without a clear idea of the future.

I handed her the lyrics. She read them slowly, line by line, nodding slightly as she absorbed the words.

Then she looked up and said, "This is beautiful."

That one sentence hit me in a place I hadn't expected. It wasn't flattery. It was an affirmation—sincere and straightforward. And it reminded me that my words still had weight, still carried resonance.

Then she asked if she could try singing it through. I strummed the chords softly as she found her place in the melody, and then she began to sing.

From the very first note, I knew.

Her voice didn't just sound good—it felt right. It was precise and controlled, but it also had this emotional texture that caught me entirely off guard. Her voice was not that of a trying-to-impress singer. It was as if she were the one who grasped the message, and like someone who had lived within the words even before reading them.

As I listened, chills ran down my spine. Her voice shaped the song in ways I hadn't imagined. In silence, the lyrics I had etched on paper lived again, lifted by the hallowed voice that gave them depth without obliterating them.

When she finished the last note, we sat in silence for a moment. I didn't know what to say. She looked at me, a little uncertain, probably wondering if I liked what I heard.

"That was... perfect," I finally said.

She gave a modest smile and said, "Let's do it again."

And we did. Over and over that evening, we worked through the song—fine-tuning phrasing, experimenting with dynamics, laughing occasionally when we hit a rough patch. We would sometimes stop and crack up when we were going through a difficult spot. Nevertheless, each round she delivered something fresh—the lip, the mood, and the clock that made the song whole.

In that small room, with its chipped walls and buzzing lights, something remarkable began to happen. We started to build trust—not just musically, but personally.

I discovered that Debbie was not only a gifted vocalist. She was considerate, mindful, and dedicated to performing correctly. She inquired about the texts, craving to know the narrative hidden behind them. She didn't treat the song like an assignment or a showcase. She treated it like a responsibility.

Then I started to let go of my tension. Little by little, the defensiveness I had borne for months began to die down. I considered it safe to bring up ideas, to concede when something didn't sound right, and to discuss freely what the song meant to me. Debbie received everything with grace. She was never defensive, never dismissive. She listened. She respected the story.

Day by day, rehearsal by rehearsal, we shaped the song into something that didn't just sound good—it meant something.

I hadn't expected that kind of connection. I thought I was just looking for a voice. A partner in my artistic endeavor was what I discovered, a person who was aware that music is not only melody and rhythm but also something with the power to heal and to bring back a lost treasure.

By the end of that week, it no longer felt like I was carrying the song alone. Debbie had stepped into it with me, and that shared space felt sacred.

Every meeting made us trust each other more and more. No big acts or drastic emotions during the process; only a constant, professional approach with respect for each other and an increasing sense of unity around the goal.

It reminded me that trust isn't always dramatic. Sometimes it's built in quiet moments—in shared silences, honest feedback, the commitment to show up and give your best.

I never told Debbie how nervous I'd been to ask her. Maybe one day I will.

But looking back now, I see that her "yes" was a turning point—not just for the contest, but for me.

Because in trusting her voice, I also began to trust my own again.

The Longest Wait Begins

The moment Debbie agreed to sing the song, we moved from possibility to preparation. The contest wasn't a dream anymore—

it was a deadline. We were given a little less than fourteen days to send a live audition video. The date indicated something very real: it was discipline. It meant practicing even when we were exhausted, making time for the sessions in our already too-busy days, and not giving in to the temptation to doubt what we had created. More than that, it meant believing—believing in the song, in our teamwork, and in the idea that what we were doing mattered.

Discipline and hope became our rhythm. Each practice session wasn't just about tightening harmonies or correcting missed notes—it was about building momentum, staying focused, and keeping the emotional connection strong. Debbie was someone who made every meeting feel well-organized. She had a plan, but nonetheless, she was flexible. Her notebook contained vocal notes and reminders, and she even wrote about the feelings some lyrics should convey, not just the sounds. Her commitment to the project dragged me deeper into it.

For my part, I fine-tuned the instrumental arrangement, paying close attention to tempo, chord transitions, and phrasing. I found myself spending hours late into the night with my guitar, running through every bar, making sure the music lifted the lyrics rather than weighed them down. This song had waited long enough to be heard—I wasn't going to let anything hold it back now.

There were moments, of course, when doubt crept in.

Would we be good enough?

Would the song resonate with anyone else?

It was easy to get lost in technicalities and lose sight of the purpose. However, each time we practiced, Debbie's voice echoed in my mind: it was not a matter of perfection. It was a matter of honesty. And honesty was in the text, in the performance, in the confidence we had developed.

By the time audition day arrived, we were ready—but nervous. We had booked a small campus recording room that was quiet, private, and equipped with the basics: a mic, a tripod, and a neutral background. Nothing extravagant, just straightforward and focused. I came to the studio that morning early with my guitar case and my nerves all buzzing. Debbie arrived a little after, composed but concentrated. She was dressed in a gentle gray blouse and jeans—no outfit for the performance, no dramas. Only her.

We didn't talk much at first. There wasn't much to say. We had already rehearsed extensively and were aware of our requirements. However, when we were standing next to each other, placing the camera, and checking the sound, just one glance passed between us that revealed everything: This matters.

We did a few warm-ups, then hit "record."

I counted us in with a gentle nod, and the music began.

Debbie's vocal expression was clear and profound, her voice steady, emotional, and real. While playing, I looked at her and was once again astonished at the totality of her representation of the song. The quality of her voice was such that the words of the song were delivered with faith—always moderate, never artificial. Just really honest. It was a performance that silently embellished the surroundings rather than demanding attention.

When we finished, there was an instance of silence. Then we both smiled, small at first, and I exhaled for what felt like the first time in minutes.

We had done it.

Not perfectly—there were tiny things we could have redone, small spots that might've been sharper—but it was real. It captured the essence of what we'd created together. And that's what mattered most.

We just watched the video playback once to check the audio levels and camera angle, then exported the file and submitted it through the contest portal, just like that, weeks of effort condensed into one final click.

"Submission Received," the screen confirmed.

Afterward, we left the recording room and walked across campus without saying much at first. Then Debbie turned to me and said, "I'm really proud of what we made."

I nodded, overwhelmed. "Me too."

We grabbed coffee from the campus café, found a bench in the courtyard, and let the adrenaline settle. We've reminisced about everything and anything - school, music, and how odd, yet satisfying beyond measure, it was to accomplish something significant that mattered unconditionally to both.

That afternoon wasn't about celebration in the traditional sense. It was more intimate than that. It was about presence. Relief. And joy—the kind of joy that doesn't come from applause, but from knowing you've done something honest and meaningful.

But the relief didn't last long. Once the high of submission faded, the waiting began—and it was agonizing.

Every day that followed stretched long and quiet. The competition did not make any guarantees regarding the timing of the announcement of results. The only information we had was that there were thousands of submissions and only a tiny fraction would be picked.

Each morning, I checked my email, my phone, and the contest website. Nothing. Days passed. Then a week. Still nothing. I told myself not to obsess, but I did.

During this time, the classes continued their standard setup, but I was not able to concentrate fully. And during lectures, I would find myself wandering into thoughts about the judging panel watching our video, already wondering whether they noticed what we noticed. I went through Debbie's performance again and again in my thoughts, at times not believing it, at times hanging on to it.

At night, I'd sit in my room, strumming the chords again, sometimes singing it softly to myself, reminding myself that, regardless of the outcome, we had done something brave.

But hope is a double-edged sword. It lifts you, but it also sharpens the fear of disappointment.

Then came the email update: "Thank you to the over 3,000 students who submitted entries…"

"What! Over 3,000!" I thought to myself in disbelief.

I stared at the number, stunned. I had expected competition, but that many entries? It was overwhelming. The odds now felt stacked against us, and my stomach sank.

The fact that this was a huge competition was made obvious by the number. We went through having national, serious, and very competitive contests. I pictured the judges in a dark room watching video after video and struggling to get the right people through the door.

Would they even watch ours in full?

Would Debbie's quiet strength stand out next to louder, flashier performances?

Would the lyrics resonate the way they were meant to?

The questions looped endlessly.

I attempted to give myself a mental pat on the back by saying that, for sure, we have already got something—a real one. The past, broken into pieces, has now become something new and nice. The risk was ours to take. We had taken a risk. We had created something honest and heartfelt. And that mattered, no matter the results.

But even with that perspective, I still checked my inbox ten times a day.

When The Silence Finally Broke

The longer the wait stretched on, the harder it became to keep my thoughts steady. Logic told me that, with over 3,000 entries, the chances were slim. I had seen some of the other submissions posted online—polished videos, confident singers, arrangements with full production teams. Compared to them, our audition felt humble. Honest, yes—but modest. I told myself that was okay. We hadn't gone for a spectacle. We had gone for the truth.

However, doubt would sneak in during the silent intervals between classes, between messages, and between the courses of usual life.

Thus, I went to God in prayer. Not only once or twice, but rather every single night.

It wasn't a desperate plea to win. It was deeper than that. I prayed that what we created would at least be seen.

That someone would notice—not just the performance, but the heart behind it.

I prayed that our work, our sincerity, wouldn't disappear into the digital void like so many others.

I prayed for validation—not to prove anything to others, but to show myself that the story I had once lost still mattered.

That the stolen song hadn't stolen everything.

And at the same time, I tried to prepare myself for disappointment.

I rehearsed the scenario in my mind: no call, no email, just silence. I told myself we had done something worthwhile, regardless of the outcome. I tried to focus on the gratitude of getting brave enough even to do it. It had to be enough.

Then one afternoon, my phone rang.

The number wasn't familiar. For a second, I thought it was a spam call. I almost let it go to voicemail. But something—instinct, perhaps—made me answer.

A woman's voice greeted me warmly. "Hi, is this Terri?"

"Yes," I replied, cautiously.

"I'm calling from the National Collegiate Songwriting Contest," she said. "Are you sitting down?"

My breath caught. I froze. Time seemed to slow.

She continued, "I'm thrilled to let you know that your submission has been selected as one of this year's winners. Congratulations."

I didn't respond right away. I couldn't.

It felt like someone had punched me in the stomach. I listen to her, I comprehend her, but my mind was slow to accept such news. It was vulnerable to a situation in which I had been waiting in a long, dark tunnel, and now I suddenly found myself in sunlight too bright for me to take in all at once.

"Are you still there?" she asked gently.

"Y-Yes," I stammered, voice shaking. "I'm here."

"Your song really stood out," she said. "The emotion, the performance—it was powerful. We're excited to feature you."

I thanked her. I don't even remember what I said beyond that. I was dazed. She gave me details about the next steps, how they would showcase our submission, and where to find updates. I wrote it all down, though I could barely hold the pen steady.

When I hung up, I sat in silence. The phone was still in my hand. The words were still echoing in my ears.

Surely, I had won.

With both hands, I covered my face and began to sob. Not shock anymore, but rather, a release. The emotion was powerful and quick, like a flood of months of frustration, grief, hope, effort, and waiting all breaking loose at once.

There was only one person I wanted to call in that moment: my mother.

She answered after a few rings. Her voice was warm, familiar, grounding.

"Hey, sweetie."

"Mom," I said, my voice already breaking. "I got it. We won. They picked my song."

She didn't speak for a beat. Then I heard her gasp, and her voice cracked with emotion. "Oh, honey… I knew it. I'm so proud of you."

I could barely talk through the tears.

It wasn't just that I had won. It was that something had been redeemed.

This song wasn't just a composition. It was the piece of me I thought had been lost when my original lyrics were taken. Writing this new one had been an act of defiance and healing. Sharing it had been an act of courage. And now, being recognized—it felt like restoration.

My mother was well aware of the implications. She had noticed my state of mind and my behavior: very closed-off, dejected, and very careful with people. She realized that the issue was not merely the music. She had been a witness to my struggle before I could trust the industry again.

We stayed on the phone for a while, sharing that moment, crying, laughing, and not needing to say much else. The silence between our words was complete in meaning.

When I finally ended the call, there was one more person I had to tell—Debbie.

I grabbed my phone again and texted her, "Call me when you're free. It's important."

She called back almost immediately.

"What's going on?" she asked, voice curious but calm.

"They picked us," I said, trying not to burst. "We won."

There was a pause.

"Wait—are you serious?"

"Yes. Just got the call."

She let out a breathless laugh, then gasped. "That's incredible!"

Her voice rose with genuine excitement, and I could picture her face lighting up on the other end of the line.

"I can't believe it," she said. "I mean—I hoped, but I didn't want to get my hopes up too high."

"Same here," I replied.

Then came a quiet moment.

"This means so much," she said softly.

"I know," I replied. "It means so much to me, too."

It was unnecessary to give reasons. She had accompanied me throughout this process. She was aware of the significance of the song in my life, not only as a musical work but also as a historical event—my historical event. Her voice had become the vessel that carried the meaning forward. And now we were being recognized not just for talent, but for authenticity.

It felt like sharing a miracle.

Winning didn't erase the past. It didn't undo what had been taken from me. But it did reopen a part of my heart I had long since closed.

When my lyrics were stolen before, something in me shut down. Not just creatively, but personally. I stopped sharing. I stopped risking. I doubted my voice, doubted whether anything I made had value. That loss had wounded me more than I admitted at the time.

But this win—this recognition—breathed life into that dormant space.

It reminded me that what I had to say still mattered. That creation wasn't pointless. That even if pain had marked part of my journey, it didn't have to define the rest of it.

I felt more than joy—I felt restored.

And in that restoration, I found something deeper than confidence. I found peace.

Not the kind that comes from applause or praise, but the kind that comes from knowing you stayed true. The fact that you endured, that even when the circumstances were such that you could hide your gift, you chose to show it as it is.

Debbie and I ran into each other later that night, and we took a seat on the steps of the student center, where we kept a low profile. Just smiling, soaking in the moment.

No celebration needed, fireworks. The quiet was enough.

Because when the silence finally broke, it brought more than news. It brought healing.

Chapter 7
Stepping Into the Studio

Where Dreams And Reality Met

Stepping into the recording studio for the first time felt like crossing into a space set apart from the rest of the world. It wasn't just a building—it felt consecrated. Right from the instant the door closed after me, a change occurred. The atmosphere was silent but tense, as if sound itself had a lifespan. The very vibes of the room were of their own making, full of intent and power. There was a reverence in the silence, a weight in the air that reminded me this was no ordinary place. This was a place where voices became permanent, where music was carved into time.

I paused just inside the doorway. Completely intact and attentive, the room listened to the stillness and silence gathered despite my breath among the walls. Debbie followed behind me, setting her bag down gently as she surveyed the space with equal awe. Neither of us said anything at first. We just stood there, still, taking it all in. It felt wrong to rush.

I had imagined this moment for most of my life. As a child, I would lie on my bed, headphones on, wholly absorbed in albums. I didn't just listen—I studied every note, every lyric, and every pause. I dreamed of one day hearing something I had created in a real studio, of watching the red light flicker on and knowing that sound was being captured forever. Back then, it seemed impossible, almost mythical. Studios were for professionals, for artists with agents and contracts, not for someone like me. But even then, I couldn't stop picturing it.

The dream had always been there, very soft and persistent. Even when betrayal was the first time I lost my song, even when I just stopped writing, that dream had stayed with me. I had buried it beneath disappointment and fear, but it had never fully died. Now, standing here, it wasn't a vision anymore. It was real.

The room was quite spacious, as I imagined, and fully equipped with both analog and digital devices. Huge speakers were placed in the corners and oriented so the sound would spread evenly throughout the room. A grand piano was located under the lights, its shiny surface catching the faint light from the ceiling. Microphones of every shape and size lined the booth, each attached to adjustable arms and cables that snaked across the floor. The central console in the control room looked like the dashboard of a spacecraft—rows of knobs, sliders, and meters glowing in precision. The soft hum of the equipment created a kind of low-frequency calm, like the heartbeat of the room itself.

Every detail seemed surreal. The contrast between the cold steel of the equipment and the warmth of the wood finishes created a balance I hadn't expected. This was a place built not only for accuracy, but for feeling. It was in the name of art that I decided to step gradually, being careful not to brush anything too soon. Debbie approached the piano and glided her fingers just an inch above the keys without applying pressure, as if asking for a grant.

Neither of us had ever recorded in a space like this. But we came ready. From the first session, we gave everything. There was no warm-up period, no easing in—we dove straight into the work. We reviewed lyrics, dissected melodies, and made technical notes with precision. Every session had a plan, and every plan was subject to revision.

We worked tirelessly on each detail, not because someone told us to, but because we believed in the song we were building. We questioned every syllable, explored phrasing options, experimented with tempo shifts, and reviewed multiple vocal takes. Debbie was careful about every detail, and I had not noticed that level of her during the rehearsals. The way she felt about tone, diction, and breathing surprised me. Rather than singing, she was making the song a figure out of the melody.

In return, I focused on the instrumental structure. I adjusted the chords for greater lift during the chorus, modified the bridge for emotional tension, and timed the transitions for maximum clarity. I stayed hyper-aware of how everything aligned. Whenever she hit the high notes, I deliberately lowered my guitar playing to let her voice occupy the space. Whenever she went for the gentle touch, I managed to find delicate rhythmic points to support the flow of the moment.

We didn't just track vocals and instruments. We layered feeling. Debbie didn't just sing; she interpreted. She'd ask about the meaning of specific lines, trying to understand how they should be expressed. I was disclosing the stories behind the lyrics and their birthplaces, and she was taking those stories as a guide for her vocal performance. The whole process of giving this level of attention turned every session into much more than a mere technical rehearsal—it was like emotional choreography.

The hours just zoomed by. We were there till late in the evening, well after the other artists had finished. The technicians were really patient as they understood that what we were after was something very specific and intimate. They adjusted mic placements, worked through multiple takes, and gave honest feedback. Some nights, we left when the sun had long since set, our voices tired and our minds overloaded. But we always left with a sense of movement—progress, however slow.

There was no shortcut to what we wanted. We weren't looking for a passable track; we were chasing something more elusive—authenticity. The recording process didn't finish in pursuit of the sound. We went over the different takes with each other afterward, sometimes on the studio floor with the notebooks opened, writing down the things we thought were similar, drawing arrows between the points of verses and choruses, and posing tough questions.

Was the emotion coming through clearly?

Did the dynamics match the story?

Could we do better?

Even when the takes were technically solid, we would go again if something didn't feel right. Debbie would always demand another take whenever she thought a particular phrase lacked conviction. Whenever I thought a certain chord progression didn't take off at the right place, we would halt everything and re-tune. There was never an argument about it. We were united in the goal. Perfection wasn't the aim—honesty was.

The volume of the silence during these nocturnal meetings was the main revelation to me. Occasionally, after playing the recording, no words would be exchanged. Debbie would gaze at me, anticipating. I would return the gaze, pondering. And in that voiceless area, we frequently came to a clear understanding. We learned to trust each other's instincts. Sometimes we'd agree to delete a track and start over. Other times, we'd nod, hit save, and move forward.

We also learned to celebrate small victories. A clean vocal run, a guitar tone that resonated just right, a harmony that blended seamlessly—these were the moments that kept us going. High fives, deep breaths, or just the sharing of smiles were some of the ways we marked those moments. Nothing extravagant. Just the silent recognition that we were getting closer.

There were no shortcuts, and we didn't want any. The studio demanded our best, and we gave it. Again, and again. Session after session. Line by line. Until each moment of the song reflected the weight, the hope, and the restoration that had brought us here.

The Sound That Changed Everything

Before the studio sessions began, I thought I understood what it meant to make music. I had written lyrics, composed melodies, and performed live, but none of that prepared me for the technical, emotional, and physical depth of studio recording. All the stereotypes I held faded within the first hour behind the glass that cut off the sound. I was not long in finding out that the making of recorded music was something more than just a matter of being gifted. It demanded a lot of endurance, strictness, and everyday humbleness that only comes when your weaknesses are exposed right in front of you.

The studio wouldn't let you hide. There was no crowd noise to blur imperfections, no adrenaline to carry you past mistakes. Every breath, every note, every moment of hesitation was captured in vivid detail. The environment required precision—this was not to ensure effortlessness but to ensure that the music continued to evince the appropriate sentiment. I was forced to listen more critically, to hear not just what I meant to express but what I actually communicated. Sometimes those two things were miles apart.

The first time I sat in the control room and listened to our playback, I realized how much subtle work went into the transition from performance to final product. There were dozens of decisions layered into each track: mic placement, vocal compression, EQ adjustments, and room tone balancing. To watch those sound techs at work was like seeing artisans at work. They were not just recording; they shaped the sound. They were as much part of the creative process as we were, not just capturing what we gave them but refining it, preserving its soul while removing distraction.

That process revealed how collaborative recorded music really is. It's not just a singer and a song. It's a shared pursuit between artists, technicians, and engineers, all working to create something cohesive and meaningful. That insight increased my admiration for the art. Amid every piece of music I had ever appreciated was a team of creatives making decisions—some instinctive, some technical—that made the music vibrant.

And then came the moment that changed everything.

We had been working for days, fine-tuning arrangements, layering vocals, and tweaking instrumentation. Later, in one of the last sessions, the audio technician presented a very close to final version of our main track. With the room filled with sound from the speakers, I sensed a change. My composition, which had existed for quite some time as just written notes and imagined tunes, was now an actual thing. Full. Alive. The playback didn't feel like listening to a version of something I'd imagined. It felt like discovering something I hadn't known was possible.

I didn't expect to be so moved. Debbie's voice, which was very clear and strong, rose above the chorus, and together with the chords I had prepared in isolation, I felt the tears come not from an emotion but from a very personal insight. This was the sound of something I had feared would never happen. The sound of a dream, delayed but not denied. And that moment, standing in the studio, surrounded by wires and dials, brought everything into focus.

I had made it.

I was no longer waiting for the right moment to begin.

I was in it.

Hearing the song through those speakers was like hearing my heart in a new language—one I finally understood. It gave shape to the journey I had traveled. The music, instead of trying to conceal the suffering that created it, showed it wonderfully, even in a redemptive way. The roughness was still there, but it was surrounded by something higher: healing.

What made that experience even more powerful was watching Debbie come into her own during the process. Debbie's confidence, expressiveness, and intuition in understanding the song's requirements increased in every session. Initially, her takes were done meticulously, but later she started to follow her gut. She experimented with tone, phrasing, and dynamics— always searching for the most honest delivery. And it wasn't just about technique.

Something in her had shifted.

She was no longer interpreting the song.

She was living it.

One session stood out in showing this transformation. We were tackling a hard bridge—both emotionally and vocally very demanding. Debbie entered the booth, put on the headphones, and shut her eyes before the take started. When she reopened them, something in the way she held herself had altered. The shyness and nervousness disappeared. Her voice, when it came, was clear and resonant. Every syllable carried weight, not because she forced it, but because she meant it. That take became the one we used in the final mix.

I remember looking at her through the control room window and realizing I was witnessing something remarkable. She wasn't just singing well. She was blooming. Her courage to step fully into the music gave me courage, too. Her development mirrored my therapy. As her self-belief grew, I started to let go of the fear that had been with me since the robbery of my original song. I had entered the studio with unfinished wounds, unsure if I could create something that felt real again. But day by day, that uncertainty dissolved.

Her evolution reminded me that growth often happens in quiet repetition—in showing up, doing the work, and trusting that the process is forming you even when the results aren't immediately visible. Watching Debbie embrace her role so fully gave me a mirror into what I was becoming. I wasn't merely creating a song through writing and production. That was a means for me to recover some aspects of my personality that I had buried before due to suffering.

And as I stepped back from each session and reviewed our progress, I saw just how far I had come. To hear the music at our session brought out my spirit that exhibited immense pride and clarity; it was someone who was very often wrapped in a coat of doubt earlier.

I had questioned whether I still had a voice worth hearing.

I wondered if I had lost my creative compass, if the betrayal I had experienced would always taint my future.

But those questions were growing quieter.

The more I worked, the more I realized they didn't have power unless I gave it to them.

The song that was taken away was, at some point, considered the last word. It had muted my voice in ways I didn't recognize. Nevertheless, this new song—slowly, truthfully, and collaboratively—turned out to be my counter-response.

It was not merely a creative assertion.

It was a proclamation that my narrative was still being written.

I had not been wiped out. My own hands were rewriting me.

The whole thing didn't just revolve around taking back my identity as a songwriter. It involved regenerating faith—first in myself, then in others, and finally in the notion that, if one is receptive, beauty can come out of loss. The studio had become more than a workspace. It was a place of transformation. Within its walls, I was remembering who I had always been—and becoming someone I had never imagined I could be.

The Work That Changed Me

Closure arrived not as a single moment, but as a series of deliberate choices. Each recording session pushed me further from what I had lost and closer to what I was rebuilding. The whole experience was not merely healing but breathtaking. The recording of each track became an organized exercise in recovery. What I had formerly composed as a reaction to suffering was now being transformed into a work that truly had its own power. With every chord recorded and every lyric performed, I reclaimed more than sound—I reclaimed my narrative.

Creating in the studio gave me back something I didn't know I had forfeited. Loss has a way of subtly convincing you that parts of yourself have expired. When my original song got stolen, I thought that the most significant part of my artistic voice had already vanished along with it. It took a while before I could again trust my creative powers, even after composing new songs. But producing it, hearing it come together in real time, watching it take shape outside of my head—that began to restore a sense of ownership that words alone couldn't deliver.

Each song was a marker on that path back to myself. I remember one afternoon spent recording a track that had originated from a scribbled page in an old notebook. We had edited it heavily, restructured it, and reworked the chorus. However, the moment Debbie got the final version recorded, a sure thing about it struck me on a deeper level than I had thought. It did not appear to be a more refined version of the previous one. It seemed to have been the definitive one right from the start. That track, once raw and uncertain, now lived and breathed through sound. It no longer reminded me of what had been taken from me—it reminded me of what I had taken back.

Gradual exposure in the studio resulted in the development of my confidence. However, it was not like going back to the original me. This was a brand-new layer, and I stopped doubting every creative decision or seeking approval before proceeding. I trusted myself in ways I hadn't before. I spoke with more clarity in production meetings. I contributed ideas without apologizing for them. When something didn't work, I didn't retreat—I reevaluated and refined.

The newfound self-assurance was not just a show. It developed through practice, reliability, and being there. I had demonstrated to myself that I could go through the entire creative process—from conception to the final product—without losing control, without surrendering to the uncertainties that used to restrain me. Each successful session added a brick to a foundation I didn't even realize I was building until I stood firmly on it.

That confidence extended beyond just songwriting. It changed how I carried myself inside the studio. I started using my time more consciously, being more considerate in my partnership with Debbie, and seeing the significant impact of each choice more clearly. It dawned on me that the music we were forming didn't only concern the songs—it was also about the process we used. There was an integrity in the process that mattered as much as the product.

The professionalism of the sound engineers with whom we were collaborating greatly impacted the overall feeling of professionalism. They were not merely present to operate machines or perform minor adjustments. They were highly focused and technically disciplined partners in the creative process. Watching them operate expanded my understanding of what it meant to respect the work. They didn't chase perfection— they chased clarity. They weren't impressed by flair—they were moved by precision and purpose.

One engineer in particular taught me more than he realized. During a late-night mix session, we were reviewing vocals layered with ambient instrumentation. Something about the balance felt off. Without interrupting the flow, he calmly soloed the lead, adjusted a small frequency band, and brought everything back together. The alteration was almost unnoticeable—but all at once the whole composition was still more vibrant, more three-dimensional. The performer had amplified the feeling but kept the meaning unchanged. This was a lesson for me: superior quality is not conspicuous. Instead, it is precise.

From that point forward, I paid more attention to what was happening beyond the booth. I observed the process of organizing sessions, providing feedback, and refining every detail until the final version was completed. The engineers were always calm and took their time. They were very attentive and did not talk much. The speed of their work influenced my attitude towards all the other tasks. I began planning more thoroughly, arriving with better notes, communicating more clearly, and respecting the studio's rhythm.

Their professionalism inspired my own. I learned to lead sessions without overstepping, and to speak with conviction without dominating. I began treating every part of the production—not just the parts I touched directly—as essential. Every step of the way was significant, from mic checks to file labeling and vocal warm-ups, and culminating in the final bounce. No moment was considered a throwaway.

The deeper we got into the album, the more pride I felt—not only in the outcome, but in how we were getting there. Never before had I participated in such a project where I felt so in harmony with the process. The stress to be remarkable surrendered to a muted happiness in being complete. The self-esteem was not the result of a longing for applause. It was the outcome of the dedication to performing the task to the best of one's ability.

There was a night near the end of tracking when I stepped back into the control room after finishing an overdub. Debbie was reviewing the takes with the sound engineers. I stood quietly for a few minutes, watching the two of them move fluidly through the files. Her feedback was given very confidently. His reply was very quick. It dawned on me what a long way we had gone—not only in music, but also in the way we worked. The day when we entered the studio weeks ago was no longer the day when we were the same people. We formed a partnership of equals.

The song we played back that evening wasn't one of our most dramatic or complex tracks. But it sounded complete. Honest. Clear. When it ended, no one said anything immediately. No energies were summoned for the purpose. However, we knew that existentialism was victorious.

That moment, simple as it was, stayed with me. It illustrated all that I could not express. The pride I had was not based on ego. It was based on love. On toughness. On the grounds of my total commitment to a project that eventually proved real, and I was a witness.

There was no ceremony to mark that realization. No final stamp or applause. Just a long breath, a nod, and a saved session file. And in that quiet gesture, I felt everything I had been seeking. I had drained my heart into this music and bestowed upon it the pain that birthed it, thus turning it into something useful. I had learned, grown, recovered, and led. I had created not in spite of what I had lost, but because I refused to lose myself.

What we were building wasn't just an album. It was a document of endurance. And after quite a long time, I experienced the feeling of pride—intensely, unequivocally proud—not just of the tunes but of the character that I formed through the process of creating them.

The Shift I Didn't Expect

The final playback began like any other session—calm, quiet, routine. We had gone through dozens by that point. But this time felt different. We weren't testing sound or comparing takes. We were listening to the finished product. The final track. No further modifications. No further tweaks. Only we two, the space, and the album we had been working on for weeks, molding it to reach the point of existence.

I sat motionless in the dimly lit control room as the first few chords rang out through the studio monitors. Debbie sat beside me, silent, her hands folded in her lap. The engineer leaned back slightly, allowing the music to speak without interruption. As the notes continued, there was a sensation that got bigger within me. I've heard the melody countless times—the demos, drafts, and revisions—but this time it was not the same. This was not just a version. It wasn't the last one. And I was not ready for the feeling it would give me.

I could no longer keep it in when the chorus came back. My eyes were painful, and I was not able to stop them; tears began to flow. Not a lot, but continuously. The type of tears that happen when one has a complete view of all that has been and recognizes their survival. The music turned out to be more than just noise. It was proof that I had made it.

I didn't cry because I was overwhelmed by success. I cried because I was hearing, for the first time, the totality of a journey I hadn't fully processed while living it.

The lyrics weren't just lyrics—they were milestones.

The vocals weren't just performances—they were transformations.

Each element of the song held a layer of the struggle, the rebuilding, and the decision to try again after being broken by what I once lost.

In that moment, I saw the clear line between who I had been and who I had become.

And that's when I understood the true difference between dreaming and becoming.

For me, dreaming was always a very natural thing to do. I had long ago imagined everything from the stages to the songs and even the recognition that came with it all. I had kept the dreams alive; they had helped me when I was feeling down.

But dreaming, I realized, was only the stepping stone.

It required no risk. It offered no feedback.

It was safe, unchallenged, protected by distance.

Becoming, however, was something entirely different.

Becoming requires a sacrifice.

It meant showing up, not just when inspired, but when uncertain.

It signified making choices without knowing the outcome, voicing opinions despite trembling, and still producing when met with silence or resistance. Becoming was the continuous process of repeatedly selecting the hard way until the hard way became the growth path.

I had dreamed of making music that mattered.

But I had become someone who actually made it.

That distinction changed everything. It reframed the way I saw the process, the setbacks, the long nights, and the seemingly insignificant steps. All my doubts about myself at each moment, all the times the vocals didn't come right in the session, and all the decisions I had to think twice about were definitely not in vain. They had all been in the process of becoming. And the album that came out was The Testimony.

Only if you have done that completely can you understand how much meaning a space can hold. The studio, which once appeared a place of stress and uncertainties, was now very intimate. It was not merely a place for working relations. It was a symbol of healing and renewal that the studio had already gone through.

That room had seen me uncertain, insecure, inspired, exhausted, hopeful, and proud. It had absorbed the weight of my questions and offered me structure when I felt overwhelmed. Within those four walls, I was able to push the boundaries of my own abilities. There were challenges to be overcome before one could truly grow. And the studio, through it all, allowed the truth to emerge and be accepted without criticism.

They didn't simply reflect past failures on their surfaces. The failures were absorbed, and in this way, something new was created. The studio turned out to be the place where I retrained my self-assurance—not in a single ideal session, but through daily, devoted labor. That repetition, that coming back to the work, rendered it holy.

It didn't matter that the room was ordinary to someone else. To me, it had become the place where I reclaimed something that truly defined me. I walked in as someone looking for redemption. I walked out with more than music—I walked out with my voice.

The album surpassed just a collection of songs; it was the embodiment of an unyielding spirit for many years, even the years that were prior to the project. The hurt from the track that was taken, the insecurity that came afterward, and the silence I forced on myself—all these had brought me to this point. But I wasn't defined by those losses. I was represented by what I chose to do in response to them.

The tale was told in each lyric we composed, in every sound we perfected. It was worked through the night shifts, the re-recordings, the times when we almost lost heart, and the consecutive triumphs that came after. Resilience wasn't something I had set out to prove. It emerged through the process.

I realized that resilience wasn't loud. It didn't announce itself. It moved quietly, through every revision made when no one else was watching. At every point in time, we chose to persevere, despite progress often seeming very slow. At every single moment, we still believed in the work, even when what we envisioned had not yet become a reality.

The record was not made to withstand the statement of power. However, after we took a step back and listened, we realized that the sound we perceived was endurance, the ability to rise without making noise, the sound of healing through action. That was a feeling of pride for me that no other experience could offer.

Thus, when the last session was over, and we had collected the last of our belongings, a big celebration did not take place. There was no need for one; the results of our work had already spoken. The empty studio was a place where I could see the same space, the same equipment, but it felt completely different. It had witnessed a shift I didn't see coming. It had held a version of myself I no longer needed to carry.

I took one last look at the room, said thank you in my heart, and stepped outside.

The air was cool, the evening quiet. The world hadn't changed. But something in me had shifted.

I stepped out of the studio with the realization that one chapter had closed and another one had opened. The change was not striking, but it was profound. It was a whispering inner conflict. I was no longer relying on success for validation. I had attained tranquility in the journey. I knew the road ahead would bring new challenges, new creative risks. But I also knew I wouldn't face them the same way.

Because now, I had more than a dream. I had done the work of becoming. And that changed everything.

Chapter 8
Learning The Business
Behind The Art

Beyond The Microphone

The longer I spent in the studio, the more I began to understand that music wasn't just art—it was business. That realization didn't come from a single conversation or a dramatic encounter. The disclosure was gradual, almost metaphorical, as if a curtain were being drawn, revealing the previously hidden systems and structures behind what I once thought was mere creative energy.

When I first started recording, I focused entirely on the sound. I obsessed over melody, harmony, lyrics, and tone. My world revolved around whether a song felt honest and resonated. But the deeper I went, the more I encountered another world operating in parallel: paperwork, agreements, legal language. Documents started to come in for my signature: studio waivers, licensing forms, and production agreements. The process did not seem at all artistic; rather, it seemed to be very important.

Initially, I skimmed them. I assumed they were standard, basic, nothing to worry about. However, one night, while I was about to sign my name to the producer contract for a new venture, something made me stop. I recalled the last instance of my misplaced trust—the incident when my work was taken without acknowledgement and without any negative impact on the thief. This recollection heightened my perception. I was not prepared to go through that again.

So I read the contract carefully. Then I reread it. And what I found changed everything.

Buried in the language were clauses that gave away more than I was comfortable with—ownership of the master recordings, a claim to a percentage of future royalties, and creative control over final mixes. If I had placed my signature without reviewing the document, I would have again given away my rights to my own creation. That incident was my eye-opener. I understood that the studio, the music, the performance—all of them resided in a broader system ruled by agreements and ratios, by allowances and shields.

I couldn't afford to stay uninformed.

The loss I experienced earlier in my journey had taught me a painful lesson. Trust in the music industry had to be earned with caution. I used to think that if two people were passionate about the same thing, they would also mean the same things. If someone had the same appreciation for music as I did, they would treat my work with utmost regard. But that was a misconception. That assumption had cost me my first real song—and the belief that my voice mattered in spaces beyond performance.

This time, I decided things would be different.

I began asking questions. I requested copies of every contract. I stopped signing on the spot. If I didn't understand a clause, I researched it. When the conditions appeared ambiguous or prejudicial, I offered my opposition. I soon became aware that agreements were not only a necessity—they were either a shield or a means of oppression, depending on how they were applied. Every agreement was a conversation about control, credit, and compensation. And every signature was a decision about who would benefit from my work.

That shift in awareness extended beyond paperwork. I started learning about royalties—how they were calculated, who collected them, and how they were split. I researched publishing rights, licensing types, performance royalties, and sync fees. Initially, the terms sounded like a foreign language. However, the more I learned, the clearer it became. It was no longer just industry terms; it was the basis that determined whether artists had mansions or mere survival.

I realized that every time a song was played on the radio, streamed online, used in a film, or performed live, money changed hands.

The question was: whose hands?

Without knowledge and preparation, it wouldn't be mine. That thought unsettled me, but it also motivated me. I wanted my art to reach people and also sustain me. I had seen too many talented musicians struggle not because they lacked creativity, but because they lacked clarity about how the system worked.

Balancing creativity with practicality wasn't easy. There were days I felt torn between writing music and managing logistics. After a productive session in the studio, I'd still be there reviewing the licensing contracts. The creative flow did not always match the mental energy to cope with the business matters. But I began to accept that both were necessary. One without the other left me vulnerable.

No, I did not want to become a cynic.

No, I did not want to see negativity in every interaction.

However, at the same time, I did not want to be a fool. The struggle with this tension was my teacher; it taught me a new discipline— the skill of producing something while being aware of the world in which that thing would exist. Every song wasn't just an expression. It was an asset. Every recording wasn't just a moment—it was a product with value, both emotional and economic.

That perspective didn't make the music less meaningful. In fact, it made it more. Knowing what was at stake gave every decision weight. It forced me to define what mattered. Would I give up ownership for exposure? Would I license a track for marketing if it meant more visibility? Would I co-write with someone whose values were different if the result opened new doors?

The questions ceased to be merely hypothetical and became real, urgent, and at times awkward. I started to realize that professional music creation required not only inspiration but also hard work. It required boundaries. It required courage. And it required the willingness to say no—even to opportunities that seemed appealing—if they came with terms that didn't align with my vision.

The idea is that the artist and the business don't work well together. That, in some way, if you are really creative, you have to turn your back on everything that has to do with money, such as contracts and strategies. But I came to the conclusion that the opposite is correct. The more I understood the business, the freer I felt to create. Knowledge removed fear. It gave me tools to protect my voice, to advocate for myself, to step into rooms with confidence rather than caution.

No one else could do that work for me.

The producers were able to lead the sound. The managers would give their counsel. The sound engineers were capable of making the mix perfect. However, it was my—a creator's—responsibility to protect what I had created, to comprehend what I owned and what I had relinquished through the contract. Avoiding it wasn't humility. It was neglect.

So, I leaned in.

I organized my files. I tracked my work. I began cataloging every song I completed, registering them properly, ensuring that the legal trail matched the creative one.

I started thinking not just as a performer, but as a rights holder.

As a business owner.

As someone who didn't just make music—but who knew how to manage what that music became.

The more I accepted that aspect of the work, the more I realized it was not a distraction. It was a supplement to the art itself. For art, in its best form, reveals the truth.

As a matter of fact, if you don't value what you make, someone else will—but not always in your favor.

This chapter of my journey forced me to grow in ways I hadn't expected. I still had my imagination; I still had my warmth; I still had my kindness. The only thing that changed was that I became conscious. Moreover, the awareness of my being gave me a new kind of liberation—the liberation to produce without restraint but with full awareness.

Owning What I Created

A very difficult lesson I had to learn in the music industry was that creating art was not the same as owning it. That realization came to me gradually, as I switched from studio sessions to paperwork, from finished tracks to legal contracts. I had poured myself into lyrics and melodies, shaped emotions into sound—but unless the business side was handled correctly, those deeply personal expressions could legally belong to someone else.

Understanding the difference between art and ownership became foundational. It wasn't enough to create something beautiful. I needed to find out who was running it, who could give it out, who would gain from it, or who would change it. It was a completely new area.

I had taken for granted that, since I composed the text, performed the music, and handled the communication, ownership was understood.

It wasn't.

Ownership had to be claimed—and documented. And in many cases, that claim had to be defended.

I began reviewing every collaboration differently. Whether it was a vocal feature, a co-writer, a producer, or a distributor, I asked:

Who owns what?

Who retains what rights?

What happens if this song gets licensed, streamed, or sold?

These questions weren't paranoid—they were essential. I had learned from experience that clarity wasn't optional. Without it, the art could slip away, repackaged under someone else's name or contract, with no recourse to reclaim it.

Throughout this transformation in my thoughts, I met a great variety of individuals—some genuinely willing to help me, and others looking to feed on my talent. Early on, I met individuals who gave solid advice, pointed me toward resources, and shared their own hard lessons. These were the people who didn't try to control my work or demand a percentage in exchange for guidance. They were secure in their own success and generous with their insight.

But for every helpful figure, there was someone else who wasn't as sincere.

There were times when I encountered people who veiled their selfishness in support, who proposed visibility in return for control, and who labeled it as "mentoring" when it was actually manipulation. Their methods were not always very clear. A few of them were friendly, charismatic, and appeared to care about my career path, but the terms of their contracts revealed a completely different truth. Their conditions revealed motives that had little to do with my well-being and everything to do with control.

One producer offered to remix my track, promising it would reach new audiences. When I asked for terms in writing, the document he sent over gave him 50% of future publishing rights. Another contact suggested a management agreement that locked me in for five years with no exit clause. They made their offers sound generous, even necessary—but the fine print was built to bind, not benefit.

Those experiences didn't just frustrate me—they made me question who I could trust.

I came to understand that depending on assumptions was not a financial option for me. The good intentions sometimes went against the bad actions. I had to learn how to assess the proposals by using the plain excitement that, at times, excites the mind. Trust, I found out, was no longer a beginning. It took time to build up and win gradually through openness, honesty, and aligning what was said with what was done.

It was among my fellow artists that I first started to see the patterns. Collaborating was quick for some artists, but discussing credits was slow. Others thought that the moment we were creating together, my work was already theirs. I had no choice but to establish limits I had never thought I would need—refusing friendly requests with no specified terms, withdrawing from sessions where ownership was not settled beforehand, and waiting for the right paperwork to be completed before releasing the work.

These weren't easy choices. There was always an emotional strain with every stance I took between standing up for my work and getting along with others. I was afraid people would regard me as demanding or unappreciative. I worried about burning bridges. But the alternative—losing my voice in the process—was far worse. I had already experienced that once, and I refused to go through it again.

There were moments when my resolve was tested. In one situation, a potential collaborator challenged my request for a formal agreement.

"Don't you trust me?" they asked.

I paused.

The old me might have said yes, just to avoid conflict.

But instead, I said, "It's not about trust—it's about clarity."

That moment marked a turning point. I had finally found the courage to speak up, even when it felt uncomfortable.

The discovery of that voice was not instant. It rather developed over time through experimentation and mistakes. I drew strength from every awkward dialogue. I assured myself by every error I corrected. I began to inquire without any excuse. I stopped waiting for permission to protect my work. And most importantly, I gave myself the right to say no, not out of fear, but out of respect for what I was building.

Speaking up didn't mean I had all the answers. Often, I asked questions because I didn't know. However, I discovered that asking for help was more advantageous than pretending to understand. It acted as a key to new knowledge. It avoided wrong interpretations. It was a way to show that I was conscientious about my work and that I demanded the same from others.

Over time, I noticed a shift in how others responded. The more clearly I communicated, the more respect I received. People who genuinely valued collaboration appreciated the transparency—those who didn't fall away. However, even when it was hard to let go of some chances, I always saw it as a good thing. Every choice brought me closer to the type of artist—and professional—I wished to be.

I no longer saw contracts as a burden or confrontation. To me, they were a limit, a framework that guaranteed the safety of all parties concerned. They crystallized uncertain expectations into mutually accepted conditions. They were the separating line between misunderstanding and understanding, between distrust and confidence. And they reminded me that my voice—literal and figurative—was worth safeguarding.

The music industry moves fast. It celebrates talent, but it rewards strategy. The artists who are unaware of their rights are usually the ones who suffer at the hands of those who know their rights. I started reading this section of the book with the idea that music is all about expressing. At the end of it, I realized that without safety, expression is only vulnerability for others to take advantage of.

Owning what I created was more than just paperwork. It was all about being there. It was all about being there with the same purpose as in the artistic process. It was about respecting the worth of my voice—not only in terms of sound but also in terms of structure. And it was about being fully conscious, at an inner level, that safeguarding your art is not a selfish act but rather a necessity.

Building Smart, Not Just Strong

It didn't take long to realize that talent alone wasn't enough to navigate the music industry. Passion fueled my creativity, but connection guided its path. I devoted a lot of my time to developing my talents, working on my skills, and improving my sound. But the moment of change came when I realized that skill did not necessarily guarantee getting noticed or reaching the audience—their foundation was in their contacts with other people. I realized that networking was no longer a choice—it was a necessity.

At first, the term "networking" made me uncomfortable. It had a transactional, artificial tone—like a term used only in corporate settings, not in creative environments. I thought that great music would be enough to convey its message. That if my work was strong enough, it would reach the right ears naturally. But I quickly learned that the industry didn't work like that. Music had to be heard to have an impact, and in order to be heard, you had to be seen. And to be seen, someone had to let you in.

That's where networking came in.

It was never a case of socializing or putting oneself forward. Rather, it was a matter of trust-building, respect-giving, and being in the right places where collaboration was taking place. It included being at the showcases, open mics, and listening sessions—not for the purpose of performance only, but also for the sake of supporting, learning, and contributing. I started reaching out to people I admired, not to ask for favors, but to ask questions. I listened more than I spoke. I made an effort to be present, to understand others' journeys, to celebrate their wins even when mine felt far away.

Over time, that presence paid off. Relationships formed organically. Musicians introduced me to producers. Producers connected me to engineers. A musician I met at a conference handed me the details of a contact at a nearby label. An agent who handles securing artists' events gave his comments on my promotional materials. These instances didn't occur in isolation—they were a result of my presence and participation. Consistently. Genuinely. Patiently.

I began to realize that success wasn't just about momentum—it was about direction. That direction required a strategy.

Talent opened the door, but strategy determined what happened after you stepped inside.

Every opportunity required a plan: when to release a single, how to structure a deal, which platforms to prioritize, and what story to tell in a pitch. These weren't decisions to be made impulsively. They had ripple effects.

I learned to ask not just "Can I do this?" but "Should I?"

I evaluated timing, audience, and alignment. I focused on long-term goals rather than chasing short-term excitement.

I remember being offered a performance slot at a high-profile event. Initially, it seemed like a really great opportunity. However, upon reviewing the conditions, I found some drawbacks: there was no payment at all, the recorded video could be used only in a very limited way, and an NDA controlled how the experience was communicated. I reached out to some of the artists who have already performed there. A few spoke very highly of the place, while others expressed their disappointment. I had to make a decision that prioritized more than visibility—I had to protect the integrity of my work and the voice I had accumulated.

I passed on the offer.

It wasn't easy.

Turning down exposure felt counterintuitive.

But I learned that every "yes" carried weight.

Every commitment impacted bandwidth, reputation, and resources. Saying no wasn't a loss—it was a strategic move. It created space for better-aligned opportunities.

Still, not all choices came so clearly.

There were unavoidable mistakes, to say the least. The collaborative EP I was part of suffered from poor communication and differing visions, which contributed to its eventual failure. I gave my consent to a synchronization licensing agreement without fully understanding its duration. I did not keep in touch after the hopeful meeting with the music industry because I was afraid of coming across as being too desperate. Each misstep carried a lesson. Some were expensive. Others were humbling. But all of them pushed me toward greater clarity.

I stopped seeing mistakes as failures. I started seeing them as tuition.

They were the cost of learning—paid in discomfort, missteps, and second chances. They sharpened my instincts. They reminded me to slow down, ask better questions, and be proactive rather than reactive. I began creating systems to track my projects, contracts, and contacts. I kept a spreadsheet of who I met, where, and what we discussed. I documented lessons learned after each release or pitch. The more I organized, the more empowered I felt.

Strategy didn't strip the soul from my music—it gave it structure.

I didn't become a machine. I became intentional. I wrote with the same depth, but now I paired that with thoughtful rollout plans. Having the heart with which I created, I still took the heart out and protected it with tools. I found that the commercialization of my music did not affect its authenticity; instead, it made it livable. It felt like a push to continue.

Purity and pragmatism are said to be the two different sides of the artist's coin in a myth. You either play the game or safeguard your vision. I rejected the classic dichotomy.

By choosing the path of wisdom, I could maintain my values while remaining in the industry.

I could protect my creativity and build my career.

I could stay true to my voice and speak the language of opportunity.

This balance didn't happen overnight. It was earned through trial, reflection, and humility.

There were times when I thought I was juggling two worlds: the one where I was sitting with my guitar, trying to capture inspiration, and the one where I was examining contracts, arranging content, and checking on the money owed to me. But gradually, those worlds merged. I no longer resented the administrative side. I embraced it as part of the process.

Because every email sent, every agreement signed, every conversation had—those were acts of agency.

They said: I'm not waiting to be chosen. I'm building something real.

And building something real meant surrounding myself with people who understood that vision. Not just yes-men or fans, but mentors, collaborators, and professionals who challenged me to level up. Those who always valued my talent did not attempt to restructure it in any way. They were also the ones who recognized that strategy was not about being afraid—it was playing smart.

The more strategic I became, the more risks I was willing to take. Not reckless ones, but informed ones. I purchased high-quality equipment. I engaged a branding expert to evaluate my brand. I dedicated time to studying distribution channels and analytics. I polished my goals. I didn't attempt to do everything at once and instead focused on doing the right things at the right time.

Momentum returned—not from luck, but from alignment.

I no longer felt scattered. I felt grounded. Because I wasn't just creating songs. I was making a body of work with purpose. I wasn't just chasing moments. I was building something that could last.

This part of the journey taught me that growth isn't always visible. It doesn't always look like headlines or streaming numbers.

Sometimes, it seems like confidence in a conversation.

It seems like clarity in a contract.

It looks like knowing when to walk away.

And when I reflected on all of it—the missteps, the pivots, the late nights spent organizing ideas—I felt proud. Not because I had it all figured out, but because I had stayed true to my growth process. I had kept learning, kept adjusting, kept moving forward.

Talent had brought me into the room. But the strategy taught me how to stay.

Independence With Intention

When the decision came that I wouldn't sign on the dotted line—when I chose independence over a "golden" contract—I understood something fundamental: independence wasn't a fallback. That was the turning point. I gave away too much of my time to other people deciding how my music should sound. One song had already slipped through my fingers. I refused to let another one go.

Walking away from that offer was difficult. At first glance, it seemed like a refusal of a great opportunity. Studio time, promotion support, and a stepping stone to the industry. Yet beneath those nice advantages, there was power that I never wanted to give up again. The agreement would have given someone else a legal claim over my master recordings, dictating when and how my songs could be used. It traded my creative freedom for perceived security. I realized then that security bought on compromises like that couldn't hold.

In that moment, something shifted. I decided that, from now on, any collaboration, contract, or offer had to go beyond a mere promise of exposure or resources. It had to align with my artistry, values, and future. I began to approach my career not as a hopeful dreamer, but as a caretaker of something fragile and vital: my voice.

Protecting that voice meant more than refusing bad deals. It meant understanding what I owned, what I created, and what I could grant access to. I began the process of copyrighting, registering my music, and securing the full copyright for each song. I handled rights, publisher splits, and licensing documents in an orderly manner. I was creating not just music, but a legal and moral framework that supported what I created.

This responsibility wasn't easy. It took a lot of patience, clear thinking, and the courage to speak out to do all this. I needed to become familiar with contract jargon, understand the concept of royalties, and make rough estimates of potential income. I found myself studying sample agreements, comparing publishing splits, and watching tutorials on licensing procedures. What had once felt like administrative baggage now felt like armor.

I learned the art of negotiation. At first, I hesitated. I feared appearing suspicious, ungrateful, and difficult. But I realized that silence wouldn't protect me. If I couldn't assert my own boundaries, I had no right to complain later. So I practiced asking for more precise terms, for walk-away clauses, for fair splits.

I learned to ask direct questions:

"Who retains the master rights?"

"Who owns the publishing?"

"What happens if the project stalls?"

"Can I exit if conditions change?"

Sometimes I would get awkward pauses in my responses. Other times, people tried to reassure me that standard contracts were always fair. Although my very first big defeat had taught me that "standard" did not necessarily imply "safe," I nevertheless demanded clarity— that is, mutual agreement rather than blind trust. If a person hesitated for even a moment, I simply turned my back and left. I realized that asking those questions wasn't rude or naive. It was responsible.

That shift in mindset marked the turning point of my career. I no longer assumed that the glitter of opportunity was enough. I looked for alignment. I evaluated power dynamics. I made decisions for the long game rather than chasing short-term gains. I insisted on control over exposure. I demanded respect over hype.

Understanding business wasn't about becoming corporate, cold, or calculating. Instead, it was about preserving the soul of what I created. It was about protecting the meaning behind every lyric, every chord, and every note. I now knew that when I handed over my work without protection, I risked more than just ownership. I risked erasure.

Equally, I realized that safeguarding my rights didn't isolate me—it empowered me.

I could enter negotiations with confidence, knowing my boundaries. I could collaborate without fear.

I could trust, but verify.

I could create partnerships, but not dependencies.

I could share my music, but not my authority.

That balance felt like liberation.

I also began to view mistakes differently. Ahead of me lay a path filled with negotiations, contracts, and legal terms. I was bound to misstep. And I did. I signed a split sheet without carefully verifying names, and later regretted the ambiguity. I agreed to a licensing deal with an unclear royalty structure. I passed on helpful advice because I didn't understand why it mattered, only to see its relevance later.

Each mistake hurt—sometimes financially, sometimes emotionally. But each also taught me something valuable.

They taught me to pause.

To read closely.

To question the jargon.

To insist on clarity.

To walk away if something felt off.

They taught me that good intentions meant little without good documentation. They taught me that in artistry, security doesn't come from hope—it comes from vigilance.

Having received those lessons, I began to establish a professional identity grounded in respect, intentionality, and self-awareness. I planned my releases very carefully. Collaborations were timed very precisely. I scheduled content, kept records, and managed expectations. I did not allow the urgency of the moment to dictate my actions, contrary to the wisdom of restraint anymore.

Collaborations became partnerships of equals. When working with other artists, producers, or engineers, I insisted on formal agreements—clear ownership splits, explicit timelines, transparent payment terms, and royalty structures. I learned to communicate not just as a creator, but as a stakeholder. I made my voice heard, even if it trembled.

That wasn't easy. There were nights I doubted myself—wondered if I was being overly cautious, overly suspicious. I worried I was sabotaging my own momentum. Sometimes opportunity slipped away because I said no. But I also avoided compromises that could've later chained me. I preserved my autonomy. I protected my voice.

As time went by, that independence gradually turned into my stronghold. I was not reliant on any one label, producer, or investor. I had created a variety of resources, backups, and expertise. I was aware that if one route was blocked, another could be opened—on the conditions I selected.

I found out that independence wasn't the same as being alone. It was more about choosing the right people who really understood my craft—not for the mere reason that I had skills, but along with the fact that I had limits—instead of being isolated. It meant building relationships rooted in mutual trust and shared vision, not power imbalance or control.

A change occurred through all these options—no to unfavorable contracts, yes to straightforward agreements, hard talks, and long decisions. I stopped regarding the sector as a danger. I started considering it a ground I could skillfully go through, without losing anything vital. I became both artist and architect: creator and custodian of my creation.

At the end of this chapter, I looked back at who I had been: a hopeful musician, naive and open. Then I looked at who I had become: a professional grounded in integrity, aware of value, protective of voice. The pain of loss had forced me to learn. The lessons I drew from it didn't harden me—they refined me.

I didn't compromise my soul. I honed it. I didn't abandon collaboration. I reshaped it. And I accepted the opportunity. I redefined it.

This chapter didn't just teach me how to survive in the music business. It taught me how to build a career with agency, self-respect, and purpose. It gave me tools to keep creating while guarding my rights. It gave me the strength to say no when I needed to, and yes when the offer aligned.

Independence became more than freedom. It became an intention.

Professionalism became more than polish. It became valuable.

And music became more than expression. It became legacy.

COMING SOON
SENECAL MUSIC
RECORDING
STUDIO

Chapter 9
Friendship, Partnership, and Growing Up

From Acquaintances To Allies

Even now, the day that I recognized Debbie completely for the first time - not as an ordinary classmate just passing by in the corridor but rather as a person with unuttered strength - still comes to my mind. Prior to that instant, she and I merely acknowledged each other with trivial head movements. Our worlds moved in parallel lines—hers among science labs and course readings, mine among lyrics and guitar strings—with no real intersections. I never would have predicted that she'd become the person I'd rely on, depend on, and trust with my hopes.

Our transformation from acquaintances to partners began quietly. It sparked in the studio, over a shared playlist on a late night, when her eyes met mine after something I played struck a chord in her. There was no dramatic conversation—just a glance, a nod, a shared sense of recognition. In that instant, I realized I wasn't alone anymore.

She was listening.

She cared.

It felt as though two lifelines had been cast in a vulnerable sea, and we found each other.

Working together pushed us to learn honesty quickly. When you collaborate on music, there's no space for politeness to soften the truth. One night during rehearsal, I played a section I believed was strong enough.

Debbie stopped me mid-verse and said quietly, "It sounds fine, but I don't feel the emotion in that line."

The room was silent.

For a brief moment, I wanted to brush off her critique or shield my pride. But then I heard it too—the hollowness of a chord played without real conviction. I set my guitar down and asked her what she thought I should try instead. That choice changed everything. We started trading feedback that was raw, sincere, and completely unfiltered. I told her when a melody felt empty; she told me when a lyric rang false. It wasn't comfortable. At times, it stung. But it was truthful—and it made the song better.

With each session, we learned to trust each other's instincts. There was no need for elaborate plans, no pressure for perfection.

Sometimes, she would hum a harmony line under her breath, or tap her foot quietly on the floor, and I would pause mid-strum, look at her, and say, "Do it."

She would close her eyes, take a breath, then sing—and every time, she surprised me.

She didn't just follow my lead.

She shaped it.

She enhanced it.

Her musical instincts were different—gentler, more intuitive, sensitive to subtle emotions.

I started trusting not only what I thought sounded right, but also what she felt. We began making choices not just because they followed tradition, but because together we could sense what the song truly needed at its core.

As the music came together, a deeper bond quietly formed between us—a friendship shaped by more than rhythm, harmony, or shared sound. Outside the studio, we started talking about life: classes, family, dreams, and regrets. I learned she studied pre-med, that she spent long hours in labs, that she shouldered pressure her way, the way I shouldered expectations mine. But she never complained. Instead, she approached everything with resolve. I began to confide in her—my hopes for our music, my fear of failing, my haunted memories of songs lost. She listened without judgment. She didn't offer platitudes. She offered solidarity.

During long rehearsals, often at odd hours, we shared our ambitions and our insecurities. I told her about the song I wrote after the theft—raw, aching, unfinished—and the fear that I might never find my way back to writing. She shared her own struggles: nights spent doubting she could survive her pre-med courses, the quiet pressure of family expectations, and the sleepless hours stretched thin between demanding lab work and music. The contrast of our worlds—mine steeped in artistic fragility, hers grounded in academic and scientific discipline—made it strange that we connected so naturally. But connect we did. In those hours, vulnerability didn't feel like weakness. It felt like fellowship.

I admired her discipline and determination in ways I rarely admired anyone. She arrived at the studio on time, even when she was exhausted from classes. She gave every take her full attention, every note her full presence. Her dedication never faltered when the sessions grew repetitive—when the same line was reworked again and again, when inspiration dulled beneath the unforgiving lights of the sound booth. She simply kept going.

I learned from her that talent isn't always about flashes of brilliance. Sometimes it's quiet commitment, steady strides, and repeated attempts.

She encouraged me during my darkest moments. There were days when I questioned whether I still had anything meaningful to give, and I feared the pain that once silenced me might find its way back.

On those days, when I picked up my guitar with reluctance, she looked at me calmly and said, "Trust the music. It's still there."

Her voice was gentle but firm. It didn't erase my fear—but it gave me courage to face it.

More than that, her belief in me felt real. It wasn't rooted in promises or expectations. It was rooted in respect.

Our strengths and weaknesses found a natural balance. I carried emotional turbulence—passionate, impulsive, always overthinking—while she remained steady and grounded. When I pushed for dramatic changes, she asked for space to think.

When I rushed a chorus, she slowed it down.

And when I questioned a lyric, she gently pointed me back to the honesty of the first draft.

We weren't identical—thank God we weren't—but our differences merged into something richer, stronger, and more honest than either of us alone.

There were times the stress of expectations nearly broke us. Deadlines, academic burdens, financial worries, self-doubt—they all weighed heavily. But somehow, we carried them together. On nights when I felt the pressure crushing me, she'd stay behind after the session, quietly listen, and offer words that didn't sugarcoat but provided clarity.

On nights when her lab work overwhelmed her, I would quiet the studio, make a simple cup of coffee, and remind her of what we had built—and why it mattered. In those moments, our collaboration rose beyond music. It became a partnership.

Through it all, I learned how vital it is to choose the right people to surround yourself with. Growing up rarely comes with a manual for that. But life—and especially music—has a way of revealing who truly supports you, who challenges you, and who values you. I realized that talent without loyalty, creativity without compassion, ambition without integrity—those things don't build lasting art. They make empty noise. But with the right person beside you, even a fragile dream can become something real.

In hindsight, I see that our friendship deepened not despite the music, but because of it. The studio became a crucible—demanding honesty, commitment, and vulnerability. And in meeting those demands together, we built not only songs—but trust, respect, companionship.

That first part of our journey—from strangers in crowded hallways to partners in creation—laid the foundation for everything that followed.

It taught me that music isn't just a means of expression.

It's a mirror.

It shows you who you really are, who you want to become, and who you choose to trust.

With distance and clarity, I see now that the difference between passing connections and true allies isn't rooted in where you come from, but in the courage to be honest and vulnerable together. Within that space, she became more than a creative partner—she became someone who saw my potential before I fully did. That belief reshaped me in ways I'll carry for the rest of my life.

Strength In The Spaces Between Us

From the very beginning of my work with Debbie, her sense of discipline was impossible to miss. It wasn't something she announced or put on display. It lived quietly in her daily decisions—in the way she came prepared, stayed focused, and showed up fully committed, even after enduring long, demanding days in her pre-med classes. While I approached music from an emotional place—letting inspiration guide my energy—she approached it like a craft that needed structure, consistency, and patience. Watching her reassured me that dedication wasn't supposed to be dramatic. Sometimes it was as simple as showing up when it would've been easier to stay home, or practicing the same line repeatedly until the tone felt right.

Her determination taught me something about commitment. I had always associated passion with bursts of intensity—late-night writing sessions, sudden creative rushes, and the unpredictable surge of ideas. But Debbie's presence showed me another side of passion: discipline. Her ability to stay steady helped ground the work we were creating. She refused to let exhaustion, doubt, or frustration knock her off course. On days when everything felt heavy, she didn't pull back—she pressed forward, meeting the process with calm determination. That quiet strength made me admire her not only as a musician but as a person.

There were moments when her determination carried me through seasons when my own motivation faltered. I wrestled with self-doubt more often than I wanted to acknowledge. Old disappointments clung to me, casting quiet shadows over even my most hopeful moments. Whenever I questioned the worth of my work or wondered if my voice truly mattered, Debbie seemed to sense it before I ever put it into words. She never pressed or preached. Instead, she offered encouragement that felt natural and uncontrived. Her words were calm, measured, and genuine—never inflated, never dramatic, always anchored in truth.

Sometimes she encouraged me simply by listening. I would vent about a lyric that wasn't coming together or frustration that the song didn't sound the way I imagined. She listened with patience, letting me process without interruption.

When she finally spoke, her comments were practical but gentle: "You've done harder things than this," or "The feeling you're trying to express is still there; we just haven't found the right path yet."

Those small reminders lifted the weight I carried, helping me refocus on the work in front of me instead of the fear behind me.

Her support went beyond reassurance—it was woven into the way she approached our work together. When my confidence faltered, she didn't stall or second-guess. She stepped forward when it mattered, reshaping harmonies, proposing small refinements, or offering thoughtful alternatives that kept the momentum moving and prevented us from standing still. That willingness to step forward during my uncertain moments built a sense of partnership I had never experienced before. She didn't dominate or overshadow me. Instead, she carried what I couldn't in those moments, trusting that I would do the same when her strength ran thin.

The balance between us became clearer the more we worked together. Our strengths aligned in ways neither of us could have anticipated. Where I carried emotional depth, she provided clarity. Where my instincts leaned toward creativity, hers brought balance and structure. Where I struggled with doubt, she brought reassurance. And where she hesitated, I stepped in with vision. It wasn't a formal arrangement; it developed naturally as we learned how the other person thought, processed, and created.

There were rehearsals when we both walked in worn down—she coming straight from long lab hours, me weighed down by creative blocks—yet we still managed to make something meaningful. When tension crept in, her calm steadied the room. When exhaustion slowed our pace, I found ways to spark energy and bring the excitement back. When she felt overwhelmed balancing school and music, I reminded her of how much she got into the project. When I doubted a chord progression, she reminded me how far we had come. Our partnership thrived because we didn't treat our differences as obstacles. We treated them as assets.

One evening remains especially vivid. We were gearing up for a vital recording session, and the weight of expectation sat heavily between us. I was anxious that the song wouldn't come together the way I had envisioned it, while she was running on empty after a week packed with exams. The stress was so thick it silenced the creative energy we usually relied on. I felt myself shutting down emotionally, and she sensed it instantly. Instead of ignoring the tension or pushing through it, she paused and gently folded her arms.

"We're tired," she said, "but we're not stuck. Let's give ourselves five minutes. Not to rehearse—just to breathe."

Her suggestion caught me off guard. I wasn't accustomed to pulling back when the pressure mounted. Still, I trusted her intuition. We sat in silence, allowing the room—and ourselves—to settle.

A few minutes passed by, and she looked at me and said, "We've done this before. We can do it again. One section at a time."

That small moment shifted everything. We returned to the song with calmer energy, not rushed or tense. And that night, we recorded one of our strongest sessions.

Moments like that taught me the value of having the right people around you. Work becomes heavier when you're walking beside someone who drains your energy, questions your worth, or competes instead of collaborating. But with the right person, the work becomes lighter, even when it's hard. Debbie taught me that the people you choose to create alongside matter just as much as the work itself. Their energy, their values, their patience, their honesty; each of these leaves its imprint on both the process and the final result.

Through my time with her, I came to understand that friendships formed in creative spaces are different from those in other settings. They ask you to reveal parts of yourself you might usually keep guarded: your insecurities, ambitions, fragile confidence, and quiet hopes. Not everyone is capable of holding that kind of vulnerability. But Debbie did. And in doing so, she taught me about trust in a way I hadn't experienced before.

She taught me that loyalty isn't loud—it's consistent.

It's in the way she showed up, the way she listened, the way she pushed me when I needed pushing, and the way she stepped back when I needed space.

It wasn't about grand gestures. It was about presence.

Above all, her force of character was, for me, a source of strength. Her support made me more emotionally stable. The disparity between our personalities was a perfect match. The firmness of her character kept me constantly in touch with reality. And the moral quality of her character was a constant reminder of those whom I wish to be around, not only as partners but also as friends.

Through every unexpected challenge, every quiet doubt, every victory, and every moment of pressure, Debbie helped me discover a truth I wish I had learned earlier: success doesn't happen alone. It unfolds through the people who choose to walk with you. They are the ones who reflect your worth back to you when you lose sight of it, who help shoulder the load when it feels heavy, and who recognize not only your abilities, but the person behind them.

She became that kind of person for me.

And in the process, she changed how I saw friendship, partnership, and myself.

Where Music Met Maturity

My partnership with Debbie grew into something far deeper than collaboration. It became a source of steadiness during seasons when life beyond the studio felt uncertain and overwhelming. We stood by each other through personal struggles, some minor, others deeply meaningful, and in that support, we created more than music. We built a shared strength that carried us forward.

There was a time when I faced an unexpected family crisis: a close relative fell seriously ill. I found myself torn between school, music, and the urgent need to be home. I considered stepping away from sessions, perhaps even abandoning the project altogether. Uncertainty pressed heavily on me, and grief left me doubting whether I still had the strength to create. I didn't voice any of it at first. I simply showed up for rehearsal one evening, sat in the booth, and strummed a few chords, hoping the music would give me something to hold onto.

Debbie noticed immediately. She didn't ask what was wrong. She didn't press.

Instead, she closed the studio door, turned off the lights except for the soft glow above the mixing board, and said, "If you need to talk—or not talk—this room's still ours."

She handed me a bottle of water, rested her hand on the guitar case, and waited. In the dim room, I quietly let everything spill out, allowing grief and fear to move through the strings. She sang with me that night, not only the melody, but the unspoken emotion that lingered between each note. When I finished, I realized I was no longer alone.

That moment wasn't the only time she carried unspoken burdens with me. She also had her own share of pressure, balancing her pre-med classes with lab work and rehearsals. There were evenings when she arrived clearly exhausted, her eyes heavy and her movements unhurried. Still, she never walked away without first making the effort to reset, easing into warm-ups, moving through gentle scales, or humming harmonies until something finally fell into place. When the exhaustion threatened to silence her, I reminded her how much she gave the music, how much her voice gave me purpose. And that helped us both continue.

Through shared moments of strain and sorrow, uncertainty and weariness, we grew into a quiet source of strength for one another. What we built together went far beyond songwriting. It was an act of mutual support, of carrying life's heaviness together, of showing up for each other when everything felt delicate, and choosing to keep creating anyway. Sometimes, the kindest thing you can do for someone who is hurting is to give them a moment of clarity. That's what those sessions became: moments where nothing else existed but melody, trust, and shared breath.

And there were moments of triumph. Genuine ones. They carried weight, not because they came easily, but because of all we had endured to reach them. When the first track we finished finally appeared on streaming platforms, and the response felt sincere rather than merely kind, I remember how we marked the moment. There was no celebration, no spectacle. We sat on the studio floor instead, backs against the worn wooden panels, legs folded beneath us, and played the song once more. Then we stayed there, quietly letting the reality of it settle in.

We closed our eyes.

We breathed together.

I heard my guitar.

I listened to her voice.

I heard endurance in the harmonies, hope in the pauses, and persistence in the chorus.

And in that moment, I realized something: this song was part of both of us now. Not just because she sang it, or because I wrote it—but because we lived through its making.

It belonged to every doubt we overcame, every tear we shed, every choice we made to stay.

When a small local radio station added our track to its rotation, the thrill had nothing to do with recognition. It was about affirmation. It showed us that what we built through trust and hard work could travel beyond the studio walls and find a place in the world. That recognition didn't change us overnight. But it confirmed what we already knew: we weren't just collaborating. We were creating something real with roots. And that truth-built confidence—not the flashy kind, but deep, quiet confidence.

Through each success, small or significant, Debbie became part of my musical identity. Her voice, her sensibilities, and her presence shaped songs in ways I couldn't have achieved alone. When listeners remarked on the sincerity of the lyrics or the emotional texture of the vocals, I understood they heard not just my words—but her heart behind them. Our collaboration brought two separate paths together into a single voice, and that union felt deeply sacred.

Because of her, I learned emotional maturity in a way I never expected. Songwriting often felt like catharsis—a release of raw feelings. Working with Debbie taught me restraint, patience, and focus. She showed me that feeling alone, without guidance, can drift into disorder. She pushed me to shape emotion with intention, turning it into tempo, rhythm, and thoughtful lyrical arrangement.

She asked hard questions: "Does this line build or tear down?"

"Does this melody lift or echo pain?"

Those questions forced me to slow down, evaluate, refine—and in the process, grow.

Her impact reached far beyond the music itself. In the conversations that followed our sessions, whether late at night or early in the morning, she prompted me to think more deeply about ambition, identity, and purpose. She asked what I truly wanted, not just as an artist, but as a person. She asked what I was willing to protect, what I was willing to risk. In those talks, music became more than songs. It became a vision. It became valuable.

Our work together became a quiet turning point in my life, not defined by a single dramatic moment, but by steady, meaningful change. I did not walk out of the studio as the same person who had first stepped inside. At that time, I carried unhealed wounds shaped by past disappointments, a fear of being let down, and deep uncertainty about my creative voice. But step by step, with Debbie beside me, I healed. My guitar felt lighter. My lyrics felt genuine. My voice felt my own again.

More than that, I understood now that growth doesn't always happen alone. It doesn't always happen fast. It occurs in the spaces between two minds committed to something bigger than themselves. It happens in honesty, vulnerability, and trust. And when that foundation exists, what you build can stand.

When I look back, I see now that the music we made together was never just about producing a record. It was about building character. It was about learning to trust, to show up, to heal. It was about making the choice to create not only when everything felt settled and prepared, but also when life was chaotic, uncertain, and painful, because those are often the moments when art carries the most profound meaning.

She grew into more than someone I worked alongside. She became woven into my journey, shaping my sense of self, reinforcing my strength, and restoring my hope. And that reality grounded me: I wasn't alone. I wasn't drifting. I was growing.

Working with Debbie revealed something fundamental to me. When two people commit to staying genuine, choosing kindness, honesty, and dedication, music becomes more than something you hear. It becomes a transformation. And for me, that transformation shaped the person, the artist, the soul I am learning to become.

Promise In Every Note

From the start, our mutual desire to create music with purpose drew us together, forming a connection that went far beyond notes, practice sessions, or time spent rehearsing. That unity shaped a friendship built on purpose and trust. When Debbie and I first worked together, I believed we were simply recording songs. Over time, I came to see that our common goals wove something far stronger than I first understood. What we built was not driven by ambition alone, but by a shared belief that our music, and the hearts behind it, deserved care and commitment. That belief became the cornerstone of a partnership that quietly reshaped both of our lives.

We spoke often about hopes—not just for success, but for authenticity. We talked about what our music could mean, not only to us, but to others who felt lost, misunderstood, forgotten. In those conversations, the gap between my tired doubt and her renewed determination slowly closed. What once felt like a solitary climb began to feel shared, as though we were moving forward side by side. Each time we opened our mouths to sing, each time we laid down a track, we carried with us a promise of purpose. That promise didn't belong to just one of us. It belonged to both.

Through her encouragement and trust, Debbie helped me see my music in a different light. What used to feel fragile, haunted by past loss and doubt, began to feel sturdy and alive. She helped me see that the wounds woven into my lyrics were not flaws, but honesty. She made me understand that my voice was not only meant to be heard but also safeguarded and treated with care.

In the sound booth's dim light, she would say, "Own what you pour out," and suddenly I heard my own songs with new clarity.

Where I once hesitated, I began to sing with conviction.

Where I once hid meaning behind fear, I started to give it space to resonate.

That change reached far beyond the music and reshaped who I was becoming, and seeing her belief in what we were creating reignited my own. I started approaching every chord, every moment of silence, every line of lyrics with a level of intention and respect I never knew I had in me. Working beside someone who valued honesty over polish taught me that integrity in art matters more than immediate applause. I discovered that creativity, paired with maturity, becomes timeless. And through that discovery, I grew. I grew emotionally and mentally—I matured not only as an artist but as a person capable of handling vulnerability with grace.

Our collaboration proved that creative partnerships can be life-changing. I had always seen music as a solitary journey: the songwriter alone with a notebook, wrestling with thoughts after midnight. But with Debbie, I experienced a new form of creation—one in which two voices converged not only as melody and harmony, but also as mutual support. She caught me when I faltered, and I steadied her when doubt crept in. I saw the strength in shared work. I learned that partnership demands respect, but rewards you with transformation. And I realized that some of the strongest art springs from relationships that respect vulnerability, honesty, and mutual belief.

Encountering someone who genuinely believes in your gift, in your heart, and in what you are capable of becoming is rare. I had spent years moving through doubt, wondering if my voice would ever be truly valued again.

Then I met Debbie.

She didn't just hear the music—she listened to the person behind the music.

She didn't just sing the lyrics—she felt them.

In a world quick to judge, slow to trust, she offered belief.

That belief changed how I saw myself. It reminded me that I was more than the sum of failures, betrayals, and stolen lyrics. I was someone capable of rebuilding, reclaiming, and rising again.

Because of her, the collaboration became more than a project. It became a turning point. Where I once saw finality, now I saw possibility. Where I once felt silenced, now I felt heard. Where I once believed the future held little more than letdown, I began to see the possibility of hope. Not simply hope for achievement, but for purpose. What we created together felt substantial. It held our past, our effort, and our experiences. Above all, it carried something honest and deeply our own.

She became, quietly and without recognition, one of the most significant relationships in my musical life. Not because she was flawless, but because she was human, carrying her own doubts, imperfections, and exhaustion. What mattered most was that she remained present. She stayed when things were uncertain, when progress felt slow, when hope felt fragile. She stayed because she believed in the music, in me, and in what we could build together.

That kind of faith doesn't announce itself in grand gestures.

It lives in consistency.

It lives in loyalty.

It lives in every choice to show up, again and again.

Looking back now, I see clearly how much I've changed.

I'm no longer the hesitant songwriter who guarded his lyrics behind silence.

I'm no longer the young woman craving validation from outside.

Instead, I've become someone grounded—grounded not in fame, but in values; not in applause, but in integrity; not in fleeting praise, but in lasting purpose.

The friendship, partnership, and personal growth I found with Debbie reached far beyond the music we made. It changed how I saw myself and helped shape who I was becoming.

I move ahead with what we created, not as something to fall back on, but as the ground beneath my feet. Every record, every lyric, every chord will hold a piece of that shared path, one shaped by loyalty, trust, respect, and dreams we chose to carry together.

I know there will be challenges ahead.

I know there will be seasons of doubt, setbacks, and unexpected storms.

But now, I don't face them alone.

I face them with someone who sees the gift I have and believes in it the way I once didn't.

If there is one lesson this chapter left me with, it is that the right people offer more than just partnership.

They influence who you become and quietly guide you toward the person you were meant to be.

They hold space for your fears, celebrate your strengths, and remind you of your worth when you can't see it yourself.

They help you discover not just what you can do, but who you can be.

And I'm grateful.

Grateful beyond words for what grew between us—for the music we made, for the trust we built, for the promise we carry.

In the quiet that follows the last chord, and in the pause before a new lyric takes shape, one truth is clear to me. I am no longer who I once was. I have been changed, shaped by friendship, strengthened through partnership, and moved forward by a vision grounded in my truth.

Thank you, Debbie—for believing, for staying, for helping me remember who I am.

Chapter 10
The Highs and Lows of
Chasing a Dream

Open Doors, Heavy Steps

When the record finally dropped and started making small ripples, I felt a surge of hope. Opportunities began to appear in places I had only dared to imagine. Invitations to perform at local venues, messages from smaller radio stations, even a handful of bloggers asking for interviews—the kind of attention that makes a person believe for a moment that all the sacrifice was worth it. It felt as though the world was offering me another chance to be seen, one I wasn't sure I had earned, yet accepted with gratitude.

But as the doors opened, I quickly learned that opportunity wears two masks.

One is bright, promising applause and recognition.

The other carries weight—expectations, pressure, and uncertainty.

I came to understand that success was the light I had been pursuing, yet it carried obstacles and pressures I had never expected.

Tours were the first step beyond the studio—beyond the safe bubble where mistakes could be quietly fixed, where every note was under my control. Touring meant taking the music into the world—different cities, different audiences, strangers watching, strangers judging. It meant carrying the weight of the album's hopes from night to night, stepping into rooms full of strangers I would never meet again. Life on the road placed our work in front of unfamiliar listeners, some ready to receive it, others prepared to turn away. That uncertainty pressed on me constantly.

The first night of the tour is still etched clearly in my memory. The lights in the small club felt overwhelming, the crowd uncomfortably close, the air thick with expectation. I adjusted my guitar, drew in a steady breath, and began to play. As the first chords rang out, a rush of adrenaline pushed through me. There were a few nods, a couple of smiles. But also raised brows—an indifferent shuffle in the back. I felt the weight of judgment before a note even landed. I glanced at Debbie, saw her calm focus, and pushed forward.

The song ended.

The applause was polite, not enthusiastic. And in that pause, I felt it: the stark awareness that from now on, our audience would be unpredictable.

With touring came praise—genuine, heart-warming praise from people who connected with the music. A young man once came up after a set, eyes shining. He said our song saved him during a difficult time. Another night, a woman told us she felt the lyrics spoke truth about her own pain. Those moments awakened something inside me I had believed was lost, the quiet hope that my words still held meaning. I carried them with me, carefully stored in memory, and drew on them to endure long days on the road, restless nights, nerves before stepping on stage, and the constant pull of self-doubt.

Not every response was generous. Some critiques cut too deep. A handful of online remarks brushed our work aside, measuring it against slicker, mainstream performers. There were also audience members who seemed disengaged, glancing away or leaving before the set was finished.

I met people who made it clear without saying a word: they didn't believe. And even when they didn't speak, the silence weighed heavily.

Learning to handle both praise and criticism became an early lesson in balance.

I had to decide: would I let each compliment inflate my confidence—or my ego?

Would I let each harsh word tilt my spirit?

I realized quickly that absorbing everything people said about my music would drown me. So, I began drawing lines. I thanked those who supported us. I tried to learn from the ones who offered thoughtful critiques. But I stopped internalizing every comment. I came to understand that rejection is not always about the song itself. Often, it reflects the listener's mood, their circumstances, or their personal taste. And those things were never mine to change.

I met people who loved our work—and others who didn't. In one city, after a small show, a group approached us, cheering and clapping, praising the lyrics' authenticity. Their energy filled the room, changing the air; I felt braver. In a different city, a girl walked out mid-performance without any visible reaction. After the show, someone near me murmured, "Not every song hit everyone." The words stung because they were honest. But they also reminded me that art can't be universal. It can't carry everyone's expectations.

The travel itself brought challenges I had not expected. Endless hours in tight vans, hauling equipment, resting in unfamiliar places, and then waking up worn down to face another performance. The physical strain was impossible to ignore. My fingers grew raw from tuning my guitar over and over. My voice cracked on nights when my throat felt dry from constant talking and shouting. On those days, I wondered if I was truly made for this life, and whether the dream justified everything it demanded.

And yet, I kept going. Because every time I thought about giving up, I remembered why I started.

I thought back to the song that was taken, the long stretch of silence afterward, and the years I lived questioning whether I would ever be able to write with the same fire again.

I remembered the person who believed in me—not just a collaborator, but a friend, a partner. I remembered the early auditions, the small wins, and the sense that music gave me a purpose beyond myself.

I came to accept that not every night, performance, or audience would connect with what we created. Yet there would be evenings when everything aligned, when the lights softened, the crowd leaned closer, the music settled into the spaces between beats, and for a brief moment, it all felt exactly as it should. On those nights, victories were small—a genuine smile, a listener's nod, a moment of silence after the final chord. But that silence often spoke louder than applause.

Touring taught me that chasing a dream wasn't about constant triumph. It was about endurance. It was about holding on when things got messy, when travel wore you down, when criticism hurt, when doubts crept in. It was about continuing even when the lights grew harsh, and the rooms felt small. And it was about remembering that every stage was temporary—but the determination had to stay.

This journey was reshaping me—forcing me to grow, to adapt, and to learn. I began to understand that success and struggle are inevitable partners. One doesn't exist without the other. And that's okay. Because growth rarely happens in comfort zones. It occurs when comfort ends. It happens in rooms full of strangers, under dim stage lights, in the face of indifference or applause.

I discovered strength I didn't know I had.

I discovered that my voice could reach beyond just close friends or quiet nights scribbling lyrics in a notebook.

It could reach across cities, across seas of faces.

I discovered that time, bruises, mistakes—they don't always break you. Sometimes they carve resilience into your backbone.

The touring life, the unfamiliar audiences, and the range of reactions all carried a quiet lesson.

Not every sign of approval would be offered with warmth or generosity.

Not every crowd would walk with us.

Not every stage would feel like home.

The world outside the studio wasn't safe.

It was uncertain.

Unforgiving.

And often, unknown.

I came to see that every step, whether heavy or light, belonged to the journey. If the dream was truly worth pursuing, it required my full commitment to the road ahead.

Accept the praise.

Face the criticism.

Embrace the applause.

Endure the silence.

And in the end, it demanded I keep moving forward, even when I couldn't see the next milestone.

Because sometimes the loudest vote of confidence doesn't come from applause. It comes from the decision to stand up, tune your guitar again, and play anyway.

That night, after the second show, as I put my guitar away, wiped the sweat from my face, and listened to the quiet buzz of the room as it emptied, a realization settled in. I had already gained far more than I had ever lost.

I had survived the first steps. And I was ready for whatever came next.

Wheels, Shadows, And Spotlight

Tour vans at dawn, empty bottles on the floor, guitars strapped in the back—touring wasn't glamorous. It was grueling. Endless travel days pushed my limits in ways I had never anticipated. We spent hours moving from city to city, sometimes driving straight through the night. The seats carved their mark into my back, caffeine turned into a necessity, and my fingers grew stiff and numb from gripping the wheel or tuning strings while barely awake.

Yet every milestone—every concert, every crowd—demanded we keep moving forward.

Sleep was optional. Persistence wasn't.

Some days stretched on without end. We would leave one town as the sky just began to pale, and by the time darkness returned, we were so far from home that the road behind us felt like it belonged to another life. I learned to sleep in seats, to rest in short bursts. I learned to carry noise-cancelling earbuds and a thin pillow, to protect what little rest I could steal between destinations.

At first, I welcomed the movement. It felt like momentum. But momentum has a way of wearing you down. There were nights I arrived at a venue with a dry throat and shaking hands, after eighteen hours on the road. I would catch my reflection in the window, worn down, exhausted, and hollow-eyed, and quietly question whether I had the strength to keep going. The energy backstage would hum with anticipation, but inside, I felt hollow. That uncertainty followed me on stage. The opening chord carried weight; the following note wavered. I shut my eyes, focused on my breathing, and trusted my hands to remember what to do. Each lyric asked for a strength I wasn't sure I still possessed.

After the set, I would collapse.

Not dramatic.

No applause.

Just quiet fatigue.

The crowd had reacted politely, but not with the warmth of earlier performances. I forced a safe smile, loaded my guitar, and we moved on. I lay awake later, staring at a ceiling sterilized by fluorescent lights, replaying the show in my mind. Every off-note and unsteady line lingered in my mind, pushing me to question whether the dream I was pursuing was worth the price it asked of me.

Other nights, though, they felt different. Magical. Unshakeable. There were nights when exhaustion faded beneath the stage lights. The moment I stepped into the spotlight, guitar strapped on, and felt the strings vibrate beneath my fingers, everything within me fell into place. The crowd felt alive with energy; faces blurred, lights warmed, and for those minutes, I felt unstoppable. My voice rose, steady and true—not because I was rested or flawless, but because I was fully present. I drew strength from the audience's energy: their shared breath, the hush before the chorus, the cheers that followed the final note.

On nights like those, the world outside the stage fell away. The roads, the exhaustion, the doubts—they ceased to matter. Music carried me. Music held me. And when the last chord faded, when the mic's hum died, I felt like I had claimed a victory—not just over a show, but over myself.

But success brought its own shadows. I started to sense tension— not only in my body or my voice, but in the spaces around me: the quiet corners of dressing rooms, the sideways glances from other artists, the whispered critiques at open mics. I felt the weight of others' professional jealousy. At first, I brushed it off as imagined insecurity. But with repeated incidents, I recognized the patterns.

A fellow musician once approached, congratulated me kindly after a set, then nudged me toward a producer and said, "He's always looking for fresh voices."

Later, I heard through the grapevine that he had told the producer I was "Easy to manage, no complaints."

I blamed no one; the music world often runs on ambition rather than friendship. Still, those moments stung because they reminded me that every opportunity carries both possibility and risk. Progress draws attention, attention invites comparison, and comparison gives rise to judgment.

On another night, a sound engineer at a venue pulled me aside after I signed autographs and asked bluntly: "Do you think you deserve this?"

His tone held no curiosity—it was edged with confrontation. Not because he doubted my talent, but because he found quiet pleasure in unsettling my confidence. His question echoed in my mind.

For a moment, I accepted it.

I doubted.

I considered quitting.

But then I remembered the nights I had believed in myself. I remembered the times I had stepped back on stage despite exhaustion, doubts, and fear. And I decided not to answer. I decided to keep moving.

I concluded that being successful invites criticism. The more you ascend, the more your actions are examined. Specific people stand with you. However, some are looking forward to your fall. It can be a challenge not to take every opinion as the truth. Not to consider every response as a ruling. For if you let it happen, you will lose your strength.

I watched others wrestle with this, too—bandmates, collaborators, peers. Some buckled under the pressure. The jealousy turned into sabotage; the criticism turned into cruelty. I saw talented people lose faith, abandon tours, or give up music altogether. Watching them made me realize how fragile ambition could be when exposed to jealousy. It also made me more grateful for anyone who stayed honest, supportive, or kind.

I began to build walls—not of defensiveness, but of selectivity.

I learned to choose who to trust with victory, with vulnerability, with silence.

I learned to rely on those whose encouragement felt genuine, whose ambition didn't come at the expense of someone else's grounds.

I learned that protecting my spirit sometimes meant denying handshakes, ignoring cold praise, or walking away from flattery.

Under tight deadlines, sudden venue changes, delayed travel, indifferent crowds, and murmurs behind the stage, I learned patience the hard way. I came to understand that resilience doesn't always announce itself. It isn't always dramatic or defiant. Often, it lives in quiet persistence—returning once more, hitting record again, and playing that same chord until it finally tells the truth. I learned that being a musician meant living through both peaks and pits without letting either define me completely.

There were days I questioned whether I was built for this life: the constant movement, the uncertainty, the emotional hinge of reputation on performance. But then I remembered the nights when nothing could touch me—when the music lifted the room, when sound filled every corner, and when my voice reached strangers and turned them into something closer, something shared. I remembered the faces that smiled at the end of sets, the hands that reached for autographs, the eyes that held recognition.

Those nights left me with hope—but not the innocent kind. It was the kind that comes from knowing exactly what the road demands and what it gives in return. The peaks pulled me back to the reason I ever chose music over silence, while the valleys taught me how to stay grounded when everything around me tried to shake my footing.

I discovered a new version of myself.

One who can rest between cities, but doesn't collapse on travel.

One who hears criticism, but doesn't absorb it.

One who can stand under dim lights and deliver, even when certainty wavers.

Someone who can walk on stage tired, bruised, uncertain—and still walk off with his head held high because he played anyway.

And through all of it, I realized something crucial: chasing a dream isn't about avoiding pain or rejection. It's about learning to carry them. It's about realizing that applause carries more weight because of every doubt you've pushed through—and that every cheer feels sweeter after all the quiet nights you endured.

Touring, criticism, pressure, jealousy, exhaustion—they are part of the path. They carve the edges, test the foundation, and reveal the cracks. But they also teach structure, strengthen resolve, and illuminate what you genuinely value.

Because the dream doesn't end at applause or a spotlight, it lives in the grind behind the scenes. In the van after midnight. In the tuning of a restless guitar. In the repair of scratched strings at 3 a.m. In the long road ahead to the next town.

After years of chasing this path, one truth stands out to me. Resilience does not come from the stage lights or the applause. It is built on long drives between cities, in half-empty rooms, and in the quiet moments before the first chord rings out. It shows up in the simple, stubborn decision to choose music again and again, even when exhaustion settles in, doubt creeps close, and shadows linger.

And I chose it.

Tonight, tomorrow, the night after.

Because this dream isn't just a moment.

It's the road.

And as long as I walk, I still belong here.

Rejection, Resilience, Reinvention

The moment I first felt genuine rejection in a live setting, I realized that the stakes of performance were far bigger than applause. It took place in a modest, mid-size venue—one of those rooms that offers no assurances. There were no promises about turnout, no expectation of energy or engagement. The lighting felt unforgiving, the stage uncomfortably tight, and the sound system turned every note into an echo rather than a refuge. Halfway through the set, just as I reached the chorus of a song I was proud of, I saw heads turn away; I heard conversations in the audience resume; a couple of people even left. The energy shifted. The room went from quiet expectation to indifferent drift. I felt the air around me tighten, as if the music itself shrank.

I stood there, guitar in hand, voice ready, waiting for the kind of response I longed for. But the silence hit harder than any critique ever could. In that moment, I felt exposed—not only on stage, but inside. For a heartbeat, I pretended it didn't matter. I finished the song. I bowed. I walked off. But the damage was done. The applause was polite, but hollow. I left feeling empty.

That night, I didn't sleep. I sat alone in a dim hotel room, running the performance over and over in my mind. Every mistimed strum came back to me, every shaky note, every moment where my voice faltered. I began to wonder whether I had truly earned the little progress we had made. I doubted whether the dream I had chased so dearly really belonged to me. Public rejection in that raw form almost made me silent again.

But deep in the quiet, a realization settled: rejection was not failure. It was a test. It was a moment of vulnerability, yes, but it also opened the door to resilience. For the first time, I realized that not every audience would notice me, truly listen, or connect with what I was trying to express. Still, the worth of my music did not disappear simply because a few strangers failed to understand it. If I let their absence define me, I would lose more than a night's energy. I would lose my voice.

That realization didn't heal the sting. But it marked the beginning of self-validation. I chose in that moment that my worth and my growth would no longer hinge on applause or approval, but on trusting what I create and delivering it honestly.

I opened my notebook and wrote: I created this song. I lived these lyrics. I deserve to finish what I started. And with that silent vow, I stood a little taller.

The next day, I stepped back into the rehearsal room, guitar in hand, not to recreate the song, but to reclaim it. I practiced the chords until my fingers bled. I sang the lyrics until my voice trembled with effort. I replayed the performance inside my mind, then slowly unraveled every mistake, every hesitation. I came to understand that the healing power of creating was never tied to anyone's approval. It depended on presence. On dedication. On the refusal to stay silent when others turned away.

In the weeks that followed, I learned how to transform rejection into resolve. When a festival declined our submission, citing "unsure fit," I didn't question the decision. I noted it, thanked them, and moved on. When a local promoter criticized our sound as "too rough," I listened carefully, considered the feedback, and trusted my instincts, moving forward anyway. I didn't ignore everything that came my way—but I learned how to filter.

I asked: Is this insight? Or is this noise?

That discipline of listening with discernment made me stronger. I stopped measuring success by immediate applause. Instead, success became endurance.

Consistency.

The ability to stand on stage, guitar in hand, voice unshaken, even when the room felt cold.

I practiced shows in empty rooms between tours. I recorded vocals at home to refine tone. I worked on breath control and posture. I studied movement and stage presence. I turned vulnerability into preparation.

As I refined my craft, I also grew more confident as a performer. But confidence didn't come from mastery. It came from the ability to keep showing up again and again, even under pressure, judgment, and uncertainty, and still give what I had to offer. One night at a small theater, after a string of off-circuit shows, I stepped into the spotlight with nothing but six strings and a verse.

My hands shook.

My throat dried. But the moment I spoke the first line, something inside settled.

The audience didn't roar.

They leaned forward, silent, listening.

And as the song unfolded, their breathing aligned with mine. Their silence became space for vulnerability. At the end, they didn't applaud wildly. They didn't need to. Their presence told me I had reached them.

That kind of connection—fragile, intimate, real—didn't come from perfection. It came from authenticity. It came from a willingness to be flawed, to risk failure, to invest emotionally without a guarantee of reward. And that willingness taught me more than any flawless set ever could.

Mistakes kept happening. One rainy night at an open-air venue, the power suddenly went out just as I was about to hit the chorus. The stage fell into darkness. The crowd began to murmur. The sound equipment hummed and crackled. The rhythm unraveled, and for a brief moment, I froze.

Then I dropped the guitar strap, grabbed the mic, and suggested softly, "Let's try it acapella."

My voice quivered as I began, but soon it steadied. The audience stayed with me, matching each breath. When the lights finally returned, we picked it back up with a simpler sound, and something in the room had changed. What could have been a disaster became intimacy. The mistake turned into a shared moment of trust. That recovery taught me more about performance than any flawless show.

Other times, I stumbled over lyrics on stage. Sometimes chords cracked, strings snapped, and mics failed. But I had learned not to panic. Instead, I focused on presence and connection. I apologized briefly if needed, but I kept playing. More than once, after stumbling through a rough verse, I paused briefly and then leaned into a solo, allowing the mistakes to melt into motion and feeling. The audience followed that shift. They ignored my slip-up.

Together, we just kept going. I had learned that recovery could be louder than perfection.

Pressure became a constant presence. Moving from one stage to the next, night after night, I learned how to adjust quickly when stress hit. There were weather delays, sudden venue changes, chaotic soundchecks, and setlists rewritten at the last minute. One evening, just five minutes before we were supposed to go on, the sound engineer called to say the PA wasn't working. The crowd was already gathering. I looked at Debbie, sweat beading on her forehead, and instead of panicking, we stayed steady. We unplugged the amplification, stepped forward, and sang an acoustic set. My guitar echoed against empty walls. My voice cracked. But the crowd leaned in. We ended with claps echoing across open windows.

Afterward, one listener told me, "That was real. You saved the show."

In that moment, I realized adaptation wasn't a backup plan. It was part of the art.

That way of meeting pressure and turning it into possibility carried us forward. I found joy not only in the nights that went perfectly, but also in the ones that fell apart. In stripped-down sets. In unexpected changes. In flawed solos that still resonated. Because beyond the lights and crowds, I had found something deeper: the core truth that I was pursuing—the heart of the dream.

Through public rejection, self-doubt, mistakes, and pressure, I forged resilience. I cleaned the wounds. I rewrote the mistakes. I kept going. I kept creating. I kept believing. And as I did, I realized the dream wasn't about smooth applause or easy praise. It was about perseverance. About showing up when everything felt heavy. About trusting the music even when the room was cold. About standing with a guitar in hand, eyes open, voice unshaken—and singing anyway.

Each stage, each performance, each mistake, and recovery taught me a new version of myself.

A stronger version.

A wiser version.

A version who understood that spotlight could blind, but also reveal—both the shadows of doubt and the glow of potential.

And inside that light, I found not only a musician, but a person shaped by endurance, honesty, and unyielding belief.

So I keep going. I keep pursuing it. Not because the dream comes easily, but because it asks everything of me. And the only way to honor it fully is to take the hardest routes, face the most difficult nights, and hold onto the belief that every chord, even the broken ones, can still carry truth.

Burn, Build, Become

I learned the price of pursuing a dream the hard way through aching joints, restless nights, and a mind that would not slow down. Touring, performing, and moving from one place to the next wore me down until exhaustion became more than simple fatigue. It settled on me like a heavy weight. There were nights when every part of me screamed for pause: the guitar strap felt heavy on my shoulder, my voice raspy from strain, my body aching as though I'd run a marathon. I wondered if continuing was worth the pain.

But I kept going.

I kept walking onto stages.

I kept plugging cables, adjusting mics, watching lights hover over me, and singing into drifting darkness.

Though fatigue draped over me like a storm cloud, I carried on. I learned that grit often appears when hope pulls back, and in those moments, dreams ask for more than talent. They require endurance.

I witnessed how dreams demand sacrifice. Friends who once understood long nights slowly drifted away; birthdays passed unnoticed while I was on the road; weekends were consumed by soundchecks or travel. I skipped family gatherings, missed reunions, forfeited comforts that once felt normal: home-cooked meals, quiet nights, reliable sleep. The cost weighed heavily. I watched relationships strain under distance and misunderstood priorities. My health faltered when rest became rare, junk food common, and my voice taxed beyond repair. I came to see that success was bigger than applause. It required hard choices and long-term commitments. Sacrifice was not graceful or poetic. It was rough, uncomfortable, and often isolating. Yet through each sacrifice, I learned to value what mattered: the music, the lessons, and the journey. That understanding kept me tethered when the world demanded otherwise.

Every stage I stood on became a lesson on who I was becoming. With each city, each crowd, each sunrise in a new town, I gathered parts of myself that had been hidden behind self-doubt.

On some nights, I felt fragile—scared that a single missed chord would unravel everything.

On other nights, I felt transformed—confident, alive, charged by the heartbeat of dozens of strangers swaying and listening.

I noticed subtle shifts: I walked straighter, spoke more clearly, trusted the silence before a chord, and embraced the hush rather than fear it.

I became someone who did more than perform songs. I carried them with me. I learned presence, responsibility, and self-awareness, and I understood that growth does not always show itself on the surface. Sometimes it's felt in steadier breathing before a verse, in calm hands when the lights are blinding, in a grounded voice when voices around you roar for attention. The stage became a mirror—revealing not only what I could do, but who I was becoming.

Even amid the chaos, with van rides stretching into dawn, rain-soaked crowds, failing equipment, and last-minute cancellations, I still found small, unexpected moments of joy. I felt it whenever a stranger clapped for a lyric they connected with, whenever someone whispered thanks after a quiet song, or when a small town overshadow lit up because a few borrowed words hit home. In those flashes, fatigue dissolved, distance blurred, and music repaid me with meaning. I learned that joy doesn't always arrive in bright lights or roaring applause. It whispers in a shared gaze, it hums in hushed admiration, it breathes in the gratitude of someone's sincerity. Every small point of connection, a single smile, a tear, a quiet nod, slowly formed a gentle armor around my spirit. They reminded me why I kept moving forward, playing, and giving.

Through every high and low, I learned the real meaning of perseverance. Not the kind celebrated on stage, but the kind forged in empty rooms, in broken sleep, in aching limbs, and uncertain roads. Resilience became less about pushing through one show and more about showing up for the next, even when everything inside asked to stop.

I learned that patience isn't about waiting for the perfect timing— it's about staying with purpose.

I learned that strength isn't the absence of fear, but movement in spite of it.

And I learned that dreams aren't destinations, but journeys composed of failures, recoveries, quiet victories, and resting steps forward.

I started to see the long nights and early mornings as part of the work itself, just as necessary as writing a song, just as important as tuning a chord, just as real as applause that rattles a room. Burnout was not a sign of failure. It was feedback. It was a signal. A reminder that I was human. Those limits existed. That survival in the music world meant learning to balance art and stamina. I taught myself to rest when I could, to recharge when I must, to differentiate between creative exhaustion and physical breakdown. I learned how to set boundaries. I learned to care for myself. I learned that protecting a dream also meant protecting myself, my body, my mind, my voice, so I could stay on the path long enough to finish the journey.

As I carried that understanding with me, I realized that pursuing a dream was not only about letting things go. It was about creating something new, a version of myself shaped by endurance, clarity, hope, and humility. I held tighter to authenticity. I weighed opportunities not by sparkle but by value. I judged success not by crowds, but by inner peace. I measured achievement not by chart placements or applause, but by quiet nights when I turned my strings, strummed a chord, and felt truth in the vibration. Each note became a testament, not only to the dream I was chasing, but to the person I was becoming along the way.

The highs dazzled.

The lows burned. But together they etched a roadmap of resilience across my bones—a map that no failure could erase.

I learned that perseverance is not just the act of enduring. It is the choice to believe again after doubt. It is the willingness to lose comfort in favor of growth. It is the strength to carry scars as proof that you walked through fire, survived, and emerged ready to shine again.

Tonight, I step onto another stage, guitar in hand, with a voice shaped by nights of both triumph and trial. I don't walk under lights looking for adoration. I walk to echo the truth. I keep walking to prove that loving music and what it has the power to shape is worth every bruise, every heartbreak, every sacrifice, and every doubt. I walk because I have learned that not everyone who wanders is lost. Some find their direction again in the echo of strings, in the stillness before applause, and in the quiet promise held inside every chord: this is just the beginning.

Chapter 11
When Life Interrupted the Music

When Responsibility Rewrote The Rhythm

Growing older brought a truth I wasn't prepared to face: life does not pause for passion. When I was younger, music carried me through everything. It was the priority, the anchor, the identity. I shaped my days around rehearsals, songwriting sessions, late-night recording experiments, and spontaneous performances. I thought that if I loved music enough, the rest of my life would somehow arrange itself around that love. But as the years passed, reality pressed closer. Bills came due. Family members needed support. Unexpected responsibilities transformed what once felt like an open, limitless creative life into something heavier, more complex, and far more demanding than I had ever imagined. Trying to balance music with those responsibilities was not a smooth transition. It was a direct collision between two worlds I once believed could coexist together without friction.

The balance I was forced into didn't come gradually. It arrived in sharp moments that pushed me into choices I didn't want to make. There were mornings when I woke up planning to practice a new song, only to find myself called to handle urgent tasks that had nothing to do with music. Appointments, obligations, financial responsibilities, and sudden crises began to crowd my calendar, leaving less and less space for creativity. I resisted at first. For months, I convinced myself that I could just push harder, sleep less, and hustle more. But life has a way of reminding you that you can't outrun responsibility. It demanded space. It demanded time. It demanded energy I had once reserved for music.

As personal challenges emerged, they quietly redirected my focus. It wasn't only daily responsibilities; it was emotional burdens too.

People close to me faced health struggles. Relationships grew strained. Financial stress increased. I found myself worrying about things that couldn't be solved with melody or lyrics. As more challenges emerged, my attention slowly pulled away from music, not because I wanted to leave it behind, but because life demanded focus in ways music could not substitute. I started to notice my thoughts drifting during songwriting sessions. When I picked up my guitar, my fingers no longer moved with the same ease. The music didn't leave, but it softened, becoming harder to reach through the noise of everything else happening around me.

As life pulled me in new directions, a deeper struggle emerged within me. I began questioning who I was outside of music. For so long, that identity had lived at the center of my life. I introduced myself as a musician. People recognized me by the songs I wrote, the performances I gave, and the passion I carried into every creative space.

But when music stopped being my constant companion and became something I had to fit into crowded days, I felt untethered.

If I wasn't performing regularly, was I still a performer?

If I wasn't writing consistently, was I still a songwriter?

If my energy was drained by obligations far from stages and studios, did my creative identity still belong to me?

Those questions lingered like a fog I couldn't walk through. I struggled with guilt on many levels. Guilt for stepping back, guilt for no longer being the artist I used to be, and guilt for feeling tied to responsibilities that had nothing to do with music. My sense of identity felt split. On the outside, I seemed responsible and reliable, entirely focused on doing what needed to be done.

But inside, I grieved the version of myself who lived for music without hesitation.

I missed being the person who felt songs forming effortlessly, who woke up excited to create, who felt whole holding a guitar.

Losing that version of myself, even temporarily, felt like losing a part of my soul.

There were times when passion had to be put on hold. Music had always been my outlet, my escape, my way of staying grounded, yet I entered seasons where I had no choice but to step away from it. Not permanently, but long enough for the distance to hurt. There were days when I looked at my guitar, leaning against the wall, and knew I wouldn't have a moment to touch it. Days when I wanted to write but deadlines, errands, or obligations consumed every spare minute. Nights when exhaustion kept me from even humming a melody. I tried to fight those moments, telling myself I could juggle everything. Eventually, I came to accept that stepping back was not always a sign of failure. Sometimes it was the only way to endure what life was asking of me.

Even when stepping back was necessary, it still hurt. I mourned every opportunity I had to release. Some were significant ones, performances I missed because my family needed me, collaborations I turned down because my schedule was overflowing, studio sessions delayed so long they quietly disappeared altogether. Others were smaller, yet deeply personal. Open mic nights, I passed on. Songs left unfinished and never revisited. I had to decline invitations from fellow musicians. Each missed moment felt like a door quietly closing behind me. Some of those doors may never reopen. I felt the weight of each one, knowing that in another version of my life, I might have walked through them.

That grief was not dramatic or visible. It was quiet, constant, and deeply rooted. I rarely spoke about it because grieving my dreams felt selfish when other people were depending on me for strength and stability. Still, the ache remained. I'd hear a song on the radio and wonder what might have happened if I'd continued performing. I'd watch old recordings of myself and feel a pang of longing.

When people asked how my music was going, I offered polite answers: "I'm writing when I can," or "I'll get back into it soon."

Inside, I wondered if I had already drifted too far.

There were seasons when I convinced myself that if music wasn't at the forefront of my life, then maybe it wasn't meant to be part of my identity at all. But those thoughts didn't bring peace—they brought more confusion.

I didn't want to abandon music.

It was woven into my history, my emotions, my understanding of the world. Yet my circumstances demanded balance, and that balance often meant stepping away.

What I did not understand then was that stepping away does not erase passion or identity. It simply moves you into a different chapter, one that asks for resilience, reflection, and honesty. I had grown up believing that passion should always take priority, that creative expression should never pause or be interrupted. But adulthood teaches another truth: dreams can coexist with responsibility, even when the balance feels fragile.

As I looked back on the opportunities I had to relinquish, I began to see that grief was a regular part of growth. I wasn't grieving music. I was grieving the illusion that life would always give me space to pursue it freely.

I had to accept that passion doesn't disappear when it pauses.

It waits.

It shifts.

It breathes quietly beneath everything else, allowing life to shape you in ways art never could.

In those difficult moments, as I tried to balance survival with passion, grieved lost opportunities, and questioned who I was becoming, I discovered something important, even though I could not fully name it at the time. These interruptions weren't the end of my musical story.

They were part of its evolution. And even though the music softened during those years, it never left. It simply waited for me to grow into someone who could carry it differently.

Silence Between The Strings

The empty room felt different now. Not just quiet—heavy. When I picked up my guitar and worked through the familiar chords, the strings echoed back with an awkward, hollow sound. That lull wasn't just about missing rhythm or broken practice habits. It felt deeper: like I was listening to someone else's hands, someone else's memory.

In the months since life pushed me off the road and out of the studio,

I kept trying to reconcile who I was then with who I was becoming now. I looked at myself in the mirror one ordinary morning and asked: If not this—if not songs and stages—then what am I?

Music had once marked my identity so clearly. Friends knew me as the woman with the guitar; my phone was full of lyric notes; every spare minute was for chords or rehearsal. As responsibilities multiplied, with bills due, family needs, and sudden emergencies, the space I once had for music slowly disappeared. Some days I skipped songwriting because I had to work overtime; other days I postponed rehearsals for meetings, errands, or quiet recoveries.

Music wasn't gone.

It was compressed into the narrow corners of a daily routine that no longer had room for long creative nights.

That shrinking space forced me to question who I was. Without the steady act of creating, without upcoming shows, without the pull of expectation, I felt awkward, out of rhythm, and incomplete. I began to wonder if I had been fooling myself all along. Perhaps I had never been an artist at all—just a young soul chasing sound, ignoring the weight of living beyond it. The stillness pressed on me. It made me wonder how much of who I was rested on applause, and how much rested on something more enduring.

In that silence, I learned something necessary: that coping becomes the instrument.

I began small.

I walked early, before the city awakened—breathing air that tasted fresh and calm.

I carried a pen and a notebook everywhere, not forcing lyrics, but letting thoughts spill in fragments: memories, fears, hopes, baseless waiting.

I wrote about the world when I wished for melody. I made it a practice to honor rest—even if the gut reaction told me I should be producing. I let myself sleep in, skip practice, and do nothing.

At first, it felt like giving up. Over time, it felt like saving myself.

Those coping habits became anchors. On days when grief or anxiety knocked me down, I sat quietly rather than trying to "beat it with music." I learned to name the pain, to look it in the eye, to accept that sometimes strength isn't a performance. Sometimes strength is silence. Sometimes it's stillness. And in that stillness, I began to rebuild.

Through that rebuilding, I discovered hidden strengths. I found empathy for others in their own darkness. I stood beside friends whose burdens were far heavier than my own: illness, loss, fear, not as a musician writing about pain, but as a human being who truly understood its weight. I held hands, I listened, and I sat in silence together. I realized that art doesn't always need a stage. Sometimes it just needs a heart. That ability to remain present, to give freely without expecting anything in return, and to care without putting on a performance was something I realized had been within me all along.

Music had sharpened it.

Life was teaching me how to use it beyond chords.

As I came to terms with the gaps in my career timeline, I reshaped my definition of success. I once believed success was linear: song leads to stage, stage to applause, and applause to recognition. But real life taught me that success curves, bends, stalls, and delays. Sometimes it hides behind bills paid, reconciliations made, or moments of peace found in between responsibilities. I started measuring success in a different way, not by the reaction of a crowd, but by survival. By the ability to keep breathing when life asked for more than I thought I had. By the strength to keep caring when exhaustion pressed in. By the grace to heal when old wounds opened again.

Letting go of those old measures did not make me weaker. It made me wiser. I learned to forgive myself for the detours I took.

For nights, I couldn't sing.

For words I couldn't finish.

For commitments I had to set aside.

I forgave the lost gigs, the abandoned songs, the dreams paused. And in that forgiveness, I felt a flicker of liberation.

I stopped seeing detours as failures. Instead, I began to view them as recalibrations. I stopped thinking I was broken because I paused. Instead, I recognized the courage it took to step off the path when it no longer served the journey. I replaced shame with acceptance. I replaced guilt with intention. I replaced constant striving with mindful living.

Music never left me. It simply softened, like a flame resting beneath ash, waiting quietly and patiently for its moment. On a sleepy afternoon, I strummed a soft chord and felt it resonate not just in strings, but under my ribs. The resonance lasted longer than before. It wasn't demanding. It was breathing. Music became less about being heard and more about being felt—less about applause, more about authenticity.

In that repressed silence, I found humility. I learned to appreciate small creativity: a humming tune during daily chores, a whispered lyric in the shower, a melody born out of memory rather than ambition. I started listening more closely to the world around me, to the people in my life, to the quieter seasons, and I began to hear rhythms that existed beyond the stage.

I realized identity isn't fixed. It doesn't stay tethered to career, to recognition, to spotlight. Identity breathes. It changes. It grows. It folds in hardship, stretches in hope, bends under strain, and rises with honesty. I wasn't just a musician. I was a human living, hurting, healing. I was someone who survived silence.

As I moved back into the demands of life, sometimes messy and often unpredictable, I carried a different rhythm with me.

One marked by patience, self-compassion, and empathy.

One who understood the value of pause, the power of reflection, the strength in silence.

One that recognized that every detour, every quiet season, every time I chose responsibility over ambition—those were notes in a larger composition.

Not failure. Not silence. Not emptiness. Just different verses.

One evening, after another routine of errands and calls, I sat at the edge of my bed, guitar resting across my lap, and closed my eyes. I let the silence settle around me. Then, slowly, I strummed one chord. Then another. I didn't write. I didn't plan. I just felt. The strings hummed softly. I felt the vibration beneath my fingers, moving up my arms and settling in my chest. And for the first time in a long while, the silence did not feel hollow. It felt complete. Filled with possibility. Filled with patience. Filled with my true essence.

I didn't know where the music would take me next. Maybe to a studio. Maybe to a quiet corner of a café. Perhaps it'd wait a while longer. But I knew this: I wasn't lost. I was becoming. And that, in its own way, felt like the truest song I'd ever written.

New Light In Quiet Seasons

When the music slowed, and life closed in from every direction, I learned that creativity does not vanish. It adjusts and finds new ways to exist. In those days, I found new forms of creativity through hardship, reshaping how I wrote, how I felt, how I lived. The songs became less about the spotlight and more about survival. I stopped writing for applause. I wrote instead to stay alive within myself, to chart inner terrain I hadn't known existed.

During that stretch, when performances were rare, and my guitar rested quietly in its case, I kept writing privately even when I wasn't performing. In the soft hours before dawn, I opened my journal and scribbled thoughts that did not claim melody or structure. Some lines became poems, others vague sketches, and some just mirrored emotional echoes on paper. I never meant them for anyone else. I did not plan to shape them into songs or record them. I wrote them for a single audience, myself. And that quiet, unspoken act carried a meaning I could not fully understand at the time. It kept my voice alive when the world was not listening.

With that, private writing came a deeper understanding of rest. I discovered the value of rest when creative pressure eased off, but the aches of living remained. It wasn't rest for laziness or escape. It was rest for healing. Sleep became medicine. Mornings without deadlines began to feel like gentle reset points. I learned that rest does not dull ambition. It restores it. That the pauses between making and performing, between striving and delivering, could be fertile ground for renewed purpose. When I stopped demanding output, I began allowing recovery. When I stopped asking for rhythm, I let silence remind me why rhythm mattered.

As I settled into a slower pace, I discovered unexpected support from people who remained present even after the noise faded. I leaned on the people who supported me. Not just friends who encouraged a comeback, but loved ones who accepted the silences, allowed the absences, and offered presence without expectation. Some called to check in, some listened without judgment, and others reminded me of value beyond music. Their patience held me when hope felt distant. Their kindness reminded me that identity isn't solely tied to productivity or success. It's rooted in belonging, in relationships, in love that isn't performative but constant.

With support and renewed rest, I began to reimagine what it meant to be creative—not just for myself, but for others. I found meaning in helping others through their own challenges. A friend whose heart had broken over a lost love found solace in a text I wrote, describing grief as a thin silver thread of dawn light. Another, an old acquaintance navigating career disappointment, told me my words had reminded him he wasn't alone. I gave what I had, my time, a listening ear, quiet words of encouragement, not as an artist with a public voice, but as a person who had paused, faltered, and endured. In that space, I understood that one of the most meaningful songs I could ever offer did not require a microphone. It required empathy.

That period tested me. It reshaped me. But it didn't break me.

One evening, sitting on the worn couch in my childhood home, I turned through the pages of my notebook, reading entries written during anxious nights, regret-heavy mornings, and afternoons marked by quiet tears. Each line bore scars: crossed-out words, shaky handwriting, half-formed ideas. None of them looked like a songbook. Yet as I read, a seed stirred. A recurring image emerged: a single candle flame trembling against dark walls. Behind it, faint outlines of hope. That simple sketch, over and over, felt like the truth. I closed the journal, exhaled. I realized music had never left me. It had simply shifted, moving from guitar and microphone to pen and my memories.

Gradually, I integrated that transformation into my identity. I began to understand that being a musician didn't depend solely on the stage or the audience. It depended on whether I remained true to my inner voice—whether I listened, wrote, felt, even in silence. I started to accept that music could exist as a heartbeat, not broadcast. It could be 'refuge,' not 'performance.' That I could be an artist even when the world didn't see or hear me, in fact, maybe those quiet seasons shaped me more than the roaring ones ever could.

Months turned into years, and the ache of detours softened. The chords I once played loudly echoed within, not without. I stopped begging silence to turn into song, and instead learned to listen to what filled the quiet—memories, regrets, hopes, love, fear. I wrote again, but differently. I wrote with gentleness. I wrote with scars. I wrote with gratitude. The themes changed: loss and healing, healing and hope, hope and acceptance. The lines carried softness, not loudness; sincerity, not swagger.

One night, I sat under a simple lamp, guitar on my lap, and played the first chord in months. The note hung in the room, unadorned, unsuspecting. I closed my eyes. I felt the vibration settle against my chest. I felt the weight of all I had carried: responsibility, loss, survival, and rediscovery. And I realized this: the silence had not stolen my music. It had deepened it.

The song that followed wasn't built for a crowd. It wasn't polished for release. It was rough-edged, jagged, and honest. It bore the ache of time, the depth of pain, the fragility of memory—and the quiet strength of renewal. When I sang, my voice didn't echo across a stage. It resonated inside me, steady and real. In that solitude, I felt more alive than in any performance I had ever given.

I pressed recording on my phone, not to share the track, but to capture the moment—to prove to myself I hadn't lost everything that I was still capable of creation. That my voice was still mine, and in that act, I reclaimed not a career, but authenticity.

Walking away from pressure meant I had to redefine ambition. I no longer measured progress by applause, but by presence.

By healing.

By love.

By quiet growth.

By persistence.

I restructured my dreams not around fame, but around sustainability—of self, of heart, of integrity. I learned that identity evolves, that seasons shift, that music doesn't demand performance to exist.

When I returned, slowly and with care, to moments of sound and music, I brought with me both the scars I had earned and the lessons they carried.

I wasn't newly naïve.

I wasn't desperate.

I was whole, slower, and stronger. I understood that every note I played now carried more than melody.

It carried life. It carried survival.

It carried a story. My story.

In that chapter, I found something I never expected: that life's interruptions, when met with honesty and compassion, can become the canvas for deeper art. Those detours, when survived, can shape humility. That identity, when questioned, can emerge more rooted. That music can still breathe, even in silence, softly, patiently, and without ending.

Because creativity isn't always born in stages or studios. Sometimes it's born in quiet rooms, on journal pages, in whispered prayers, and in gentle acceptance. And when it is, it carries truth that echoes far beyond applause.

A New Silence, A Renewed Self

When the world slowed, and the rush of ambition eased, I began to welcome a calmer, more intentional version of myself. I replaced frantic rehearsals with quiet mornings. I set aside last-minute performances for long walks and hushed reflection. I learned that life does not always ask us to move fast. Sometimes it asked for patience, space, and quiet. That shift didn't feel graceful. It felt awkward at first. My fingers itched for strings, my mind longed for melodies. But the stillness invited something different: clarity. In that clarity, I saw not who I was before—but who I could become.

A better version. A whole version.

This slower pace reshaped my relationship with time. Where I once measured days by gigs and lyrics, I began to measure them by moments instead: the warmth of morning sun on my face, coffee shared with family, and evenings spent talking with friends.

I started valuing presence over productivity.

I didn't need to fill every silence with sound.

Sometimes silence itself spoke louder than any chorus.

I learned that growth doesn't always announce itself with applause or output.

Sometimes it unfolds quietly, in unspoken changes in posture, in softer reactions, in steadier breaths. I let that slower rhythm become my new foundation.

Through that transformation, I recognized something deeper: identity evolves. I didn't vanish when the spotlight dimmed, and I didn't vanish when stages went silent. I changed. I matured. I adapted. The person who once defined himself by songs and shows quietly reshaped into someone defined by values, by empathy, by inner strength. I discovered that identity isn't fixed. It isn't determined by the number of performances, the volume of applause, or the stream counts of a song. It is shaped by integrity, by heart, by how you move through the world when no one is watching. And so I began to meet myself again, not as "the musician," but simply as me, free of labels and grounded in my truth.

In those months of quiet, I felt music living inside me even when life got heavy. I realized that music didn't belong only to rooms with amplified speakers or crowded venues. It belonged to every heartbeat, every breath, and every memory.

In the early morning silence, I heard chords in the birdsong.

In the rain tapping on the roof, I sensed rhythm. In conversations with loved ones, I witnessed melody.

Music became less about performance and more about presence— an inner hum that carried me even when external noise faded.

I didn't need a mic. I didn't need a stage. I needed silence, reflection, and openness. And in that space, music lived.

Healing found me in reflection. I closed my eyes and allowed memories to surface—not for nostalgia, but for understanding. I remembered the nights I chased applause, the times I sacrificed rest for rehearsals, the moments I sacrificed relationships for ambition. I felt the weight of every choice. I grieved what I had lost: sleep, stability, childhood simplicity. But in that grief, I discovered perspective. I came to understand that every path carries a cost, every dream asks for its price, and survival often requires surrender. I began to forgive myself for those costs, not as excuses, but as honest acknowledgment. I did the best I could at the time, with the tools I had. Forgiveness softened guilt, cleared space in my heart, and allowed healing to grow.

Through quiet reflection, I found my way back to gratitude. I began to recognize the people who stood beside me all along. The encouraging voices, the friendships that never wavered, the family who stayed up waiting when I came home late from a gig, and the friends who checked in even when I drifted away from the creative world. I remembered simple joys: laughter over shared meals, quiet nights under the stars, conversations that didn't ask for performance or recognition. I remembered that before the stage, before the spotlight, there were people who loved me—not for what I did, but for who I was. That memory strengthened me, rooted me, and reminded me that success isn't always measured by applause. Sometimes it's measured by connection, support, and love.

Those years of silence, loss, and reflection shaped my maturity more than any tour, any studio session, any performance ever could. I learned boundaries. I practiced self-care. I learned when to step back, pause, and rest. I learned that stamina is not only physical, but also emotional, spiritual, and mental. I came to see that true artistry carries more than talent. It carries wisdom, humility, and resilience. I did not mature into someone shaped for fame, but into someone grounded for life.

As I allowed that inner growth to take root, I began to reconnect with art in a different way. I wrote again—slowly, gently, unhurriedly. Songs emerged not from pressure, but from observation, from silence, from reflection. Lyrics echoed maturity, empathy, and experience. The music felt deeper, stripped of flash and trends, rooted in honesty. It wasn't created for charts or applause. It existed to tell the truth and to heal. Pieces I once abandoned now resurfaced with new insight. Where I used to chase perfection, I now pursue sincerity. Where I once strived for recognition, I now honor meaning.

That return wasn't dramatic. There was no grand "comeback." No high-profile shows or chart listings were waiting. Instead, there were minor sessions—recordings done at home, acoustic sets for a close friend, a quiet studio day just to test a melody. But in those small moments, I felt something crucial: alignment. I felt that my music didn't have to announce itself with sound. It could live quietly, steadily, meaningfully. And that realization brought peace—a peace more profound than applause, stronger than ambition.

Eventually, I realized that those years shaped not just my music but also my connection to my art. The songs I wrote after that carried real weight, not because I was trying to prove anything, but because I wanted to speak honestly. I came to understand that art is not always about productivity or recognition. Sometimes it is simply about finding your true meaning. Sometimes it's about honesty, vulnerability, healing. Sometimes it's about surviving, reflecting, and rising again. I began to create not for fame, but for authenticity—for meaning, for hope, for heart. I began to understand that real art doesn't demand applause. It requires sincerity—even silence.

And in embracing that new self, I found freedom. Freedom to create when I was ready. Freedom to rest when I needed it. Freedom to evolve without fear. Freedom to define success on my own terms. I wasn't chasing charts anymore. I was not pursuing applause. I was pursuing growth, balance, and peace. I wanted a life where music did not take everything from me, but instead fit naturally into it. A life where art was not my entire identity, but one meaningful part of who I am. A life where being human mattered more than being heard.

As I reflect on those seasons now, I see them not as detours or derailments, but as necessary chapters. Chapters that grounded ambition in reality, shaped patience in urgency, and built depth in silence. They prepared me for whatever came next—not just as a musician, but as a person capable of living beyond applause. They taught me that identity is not shaped in the spotlight, but in the quiet shadows. That a voice is not only what you project outward, but what you hold within, that music is more than performance. It is a way of being. That art isn't always loud. Sometimes it whispers. And sometimes those whispers carry more truth than any roar.

So now, when I pick up my guitar, I don't hold expectations. I hold gratitude.

I don't demand perfection. I offer presence.

I don't chase recognition. I chase meaning.

Because I know, after all the silence and reflection, that music doesn't need to prove itself. It just needs to be real. And so, do I.

Chapter 12
Returning to My Voice

Awakening The Voice Within

Some mornings, when the world still slumbered, and the sky bore the thin blue promise of dawn, I realized I had reached a turning point. The ache of absence had grown too familiar, too sharp. The place in my hands that once hummed with guitar strings had gone quiet, and it no longer felt like something temporary. It felt like a loss. But more than that, it felt incomplete. In those quiet moments, I understood I could no longer avoid what had always been part of me. I had to return to music, not from desperation, but because it was essential. I needed to give breath back to the part of me that would not disappear.

It wasn't a dramatic decision. It didn't involve deadlines or declarations. I didn't post on social media or announce a comeback. Instead, I closed my eyes one morning, ran my fingers over the cracked wood of my old guitar, and listened. I heard memory in the grain. I sensed old rhythms still lingering beneath the dust, waiting patiently. Then a quiet voice rose inside me, gentle but unwavering, reminding me that my story was not finished. That was my story, however fragmented it felt, still deserved melody. Returning to music wasn't reclaiming what I lost. It was acknowledging what had lived all along, even in silence.

When I finally allowed myself to listen, I understood something essential. My voice had changed, and so had I. Time had moved on since the last song I wrote. Years of hardship, loss, waiting, and growth had layered beneath my ribs. Those layers shaped my breath, deepened my heart, and altered the way I connected to sound. The voice that came back wouldn't match the voice that had left. It carried a different weight, a different memory. The sharp clarity and youthful urgency were gone, replaced by something calmer and more layered. It was a voice shaped by life, softened through pain, and strengthened by resolve.

I strummed the first chord and felt it slide through me differently. Where it once echoed with youthful hope, I now heard history, not in despair, but in truth. The chord didn't demand attention. It asked for honesty. My breath caught for a moment, not from nerves, but from recognition. I understood then that I was no longer the person who had first touched those strings. I carried scars, doubts, and lessons, along with resilience, patience, and compassion. The guitar no longer felt heavy. It felt like home.

I returned to music not as the girl who started, but as the woman I had become. The lines between past and present were no longer shadows to regret, but bridges to cross. Where I once searched outward for validation from crowds, applause, and recognition, I now turned inward. I didn't need the spotlight. I needed the rhythm that awakened in silence. I didn't need validation from the industry. I needed validation from my own heart. And that made all the difference.

Free from external pressure, I rediscovered joy in creating for myself. I wrote songs late at night, not for release, but for my relief. I hummed melodies on walks, whispered lyrics into the wind, and strummed chords on rainy afternoons. I allowed mistakes. I allowed uncertainty. I wrote when my heart was raw, when emotions lay scattered across pages, in fear and hope and sorrow. Those songs didn't have to be perfect. They only had to be real.

In that process, music became less a performance and more a companion.

On nights when doubt crept in, I didn't wait for applause—I waited for truth.

On days when the world demanded weight, I carried melody.

On mornings heavy with tasks, I let a soft chord remind me who I was beneath the roles I carried.

The joy wasn't loud; it was gentle, steady, and quiet. It wasn't about reaching ears or charts—it was about touching life, my life, all over again.

Returning to the studio one afternoon felt different. The walls were the same, the equipment unchanged. But I was not. As I plugged in the cables, adjusted the mic, and tuned the strings, I sensed the shift. I wasn't performing to impress. I was recording to heal. I sang gently, listened closely, and let go of the need for perfection. When the playback came, I heard a version of myself that felt honest. It wasn't polished or flawless—but it was real, raw in some places, vulnerable in others, and whole in a way I hadn't known before.

That recording became a testament. Not to talent reclaimed. But to the purpose rediscovered. I didn't release it to the public for months that followed. I sat with it quietly, listened to it when the world was still, lived with it when doubts returned. Every time I played it, I felt clarity washing through me: this was not a comeback. It was a continuation. Not a revival of who I once was, but the emergence of who I chose to be now.

As I reconnected with friends and fellow musicians, I felt a quiet distance—not rooted in shame, but in peace. I no longer chased their applause; I wanted their understanding. The need for validation through recognition had fallen away.

I needed the quiet nod that says: I see you. I hear you. I know you.

And I gave it back to them.

Collaboration returned—but this time, it moved at my pace. I stepped into sessions with clear boundaries, asked the hard questions before committing, and shared melodies only when they felt ready. No rush. No pressure. Just intention guiding every choice. I rediscovered that creative control didn't always mean pushing forward. Sometimes it meant pausing, listening, honoring the pace only my heart could set.

There were days when old doubts returned:

What if the world has moved on?

What if the industry no longer listens to soft voices?

What if the songs I write now never reach the heights of past ambition?

But I found a new answer: what if I don't need them to?

What if I only need honesty?

What if I only need to speak my truth and let it rest where it lands?

That shift in perspective changed everything. I stopped chasing millions and began pursuing meaning. I exchanged numbers for moments, metrics for memories, and applause for something far more lasting—authenticity.

In choosing that path, I reclaimed confidence stolen years earlier. Not in arrogance or entitlement—but in quiet strength. I trusted the version of me who had survived silence, transitions, losses, and waiting. I trusted the hands that trembled then, but now held strings without fear. I trusted the heart that wore scars but still opened to melody. I trusted the spirit that refused to go silent even when the world insisted on silence.

My story—even the painful parts—felt meaningful again. The betrayal, the hiatus, the doubts weren't wounds to conceal; they were chapters to acknowledge, carry, and honor. They shaped empathy, maturity, and depth. They shaped an artist not defined by perfection, but by perseverance. They shaped someone capable of reaching not just for notes, but for truth.

One evening, sitting alone and strumming into the quiet night, I realized something clearly: resilience had become my greatest instrument. Not the pick, not the mic, not the glow of studio lights—but resilience itself. The strength to rise, to pause, to bend, to heal, and to return. That instrument didn't amplify sound. It amplified my soul. It resonated beneath the ears of critics. It resonated inside the chambers of my own heart.

Reflecting on it all now, I recognize how every season had its impact on me—the fierce eagerness of the young, the excruciating stillness of the diversion, the gradual restoration in the darkness, and ultimately the blooming of the passion.

I accept all of it—the shine, the storms, the scars, the songs.

And I step forward with clarity. Not chasing validation. Not chasing applause and not chasing a fantasy, but carrying a rhythm rooted in truth, integrity, and tenderness.

I don't know where this chapter ends. I don't know what doors will open, or what crowds will hear. But I know this: I am returning not to prove, but to express; not to compete, but to belong.

I am coming home—not to a stage, but to my voice. And that feels like everything.

Resilience, Story, And A Voice Reclaimed

The moment I rejoined my guitar after several years of silence, the old strings sang under my calloused fingers, and something that I thought was gone for good stirred inside me. That flash wasn't hope as I used to know it. It was memory and strength wrapped into a single chord. In that moment, I understood the journey ahead: I was not simply returning to music. I was reclaiming confidence stolen years earlier, repurposing pain into purpose, and rebuilding a voice forged by hardship and perseverance.

Confidence had been fragile for a long time. The loss of songs, chances, and guidance made every riff played by me feel empty— like sounding like someone else's idea of what I should be. I questioned every word. I doubted every single note. But when I decided to return to music, I entered with those doubts still weighing heavily on my heart.

But stepping back into creative space forced me to confront the fear: Could I still deliver?

Did I still belong?

The only answer I had was silence—and inside that silence I discovered something new: I still carried the thread.

The thread of my own story, my own pain, and the lessons learned in absence.

That realization rekindled confidence—not the brash kind, but the kind born of survival.

Step by step, I began making new songs. Writing down the notes was the first thing to do—a midnight humming chord, a quiet tune coming while going home, and a rain Miss singer. Then words. Stories. Pieces of life I had once hidden behind tough metaphors and hopeful chords. I wrote about grief, longing, heartbreak, resilience, and quiet redemption. I wrote about the nights I felt abandoned by hope, and the mornings I chose to rise anyway. Little by little, I got to know that my story—every hurting piece, every splitting sorrow, every silence—was worth sharing. Not for the reason I was asking for a standing ovation. But because it was sincere. Because it was genuine. Because it could possibly affect other people's lives by making them feel less isolated.

That awareness changed the song of my heart. I stopped playing with the imperfections and hiding the scars with fabulous production. Instead, I welcomed the flaws: the broken breaths that kept hanging before a chorus, the unrefined harmonies torn by feelings, and the soft pauses in between lyrics that were heavy with meaning. Those imperfect rhythms didn't weaken the music. They grounded it. They carried truth. I recognized that I didn't need to reach perfection. I needed to share authenticity. And in authenticity, I found power.

Resilience became my greatest instrument—more than guitar strings, microphones, or studio lights. Resilience was the quiet voice that kept me writing even after rejection, the steady breath that carried me through uncertainty, the inner compass that refused to let me bow out when the world turned away. Every detour, every season of waiting, and every moment of silence strengthened that instrument. It was shaped through hardship until it resonated with clarity and purpose.

I learned that resilience doesn't demand a spotlight. It doesn't require applause. It asks only for endurance, for presence, for commitment to truth—even when no one listens. I started to play for that truth. My initial reason for singing was not to show my skills, but rather to get myself healed. And with every voice recording, every lyric penned down, every melody created from reminiscence and desire, I sensed resilience vibrating in me—constant, genuine, and indestructible.

Embracing every season of my life meant honoring each chapter, both bright and difficult. I no longer viewed the past as something stuck on repeat or broken. Instead, I began to see it as the foundation beneath me. The years shaped by youth and ambition, the painful seasons marked by loss and silence, and the quieter times of rebuilding all became layers of who I am today. I carried lesson after lesson: about patience, about boundaries, about waiting without giving up; about grieving without losing self; about hope without denial; about rebuilding without pressure. Those lessons didn't make the journey easier. They made it richer, deeper, and more human.

In creating new music, I didn't run away from that history. I embraced it. A verse might recall a wound. A chorus might echo a prayer. A bridge could stretch across memory toward redemption. I began to see my songs as threads woven through time, connecting sorrow to hope, silence to sound, and despair to belief. The voice I used regained texture, depth, and vulnerability. It didn't hide scars. It carried them. And somehow, that carrying felt like strength.

As I observed the industry again from a distance and on my own terms, I came to understand something essential: success is not defined solely by charts and accolades. Success also belongs to survival and truth. To the ability to stand in your story, own it, sing it, and let it breathe. I wrote for myself first. I wrote for the little version of me who held a tattered notebook and dreamed in chords.

I wrote for the woman I had become—weathered, wiser, unafraid to be broken and whole in the same breath. I wrote for anyone listening for honesty.

When the songs finally came together, I recorded them not for validation, but because I owed it to my journey. I recorded to mark return, to mark growth, to mark resilience. I recorded a voice reshaped by years, by trials, by patience, by change. And when the playback filled the room, I didn't feel pressure. I felt relief. I felt a sense of completion, not of a project, but of a circle closing. The confidence I once lost had found its way back, not perfect, but grounded, sincere, and alive.

Returning wasn't a revival of the old ambition. It was a new beginning. I wasn't chasing fame or approval. I was chasing clarity, presence, and authenticity. I permitted myself to move slowly. To honor my pace. To let songs breathe before releasing them. To let my voice grow before projecting it. I refused to be rushed by expectations, not from others, but from past versions of myself. I no longer measured worth by popularity. Instead, I measured it by integrity.

That redefinition of success changed everything. I stopped asking, "Will they like this?"

I asked instead, "Is this true to me?"

I didn't chase trends or external approval. I chased honesty. I chased resonance. I chased meaning.

And with that pursuit came peace—quiet, steady, unwavering.

When I stood again in front of a crowd—small, humble, intimate—I didn't feel the tremor of doubt. I felt grounded. Because I no longer relied on applause. I relied on truth. I relied on resilience. I relied on the knowledge that my story mattered. Not for fame. For healing. For connection. For life.

Music had once slipped away from me through silence, detours, and doubt. Now, I reclaimed it not as a means of recognition, but as a vessel for truth. I reclaimed my voice not as a performer's demand, but as a human expression of honesty. I reclaimed my journey—not as a chase, but as a path. A path defined by survival. By scars. By stories. By resilience.

And as I strummed the final chord of that first new song, I realized I wasn't ending anything. I was beginning again. Different. Wiser. Stronger. More myself than ever. Because this time, the voice that sang was forged not only in talent, but in trials, truths, and time.

Coming Home On My Own Terms

Once more, I entered the aged studio carrying merely a guitar case that had seen better days and a heart full of apprehension. The atmosphere was identical to that of the previous ones—wood, cables, and a slight, pleasant sourness of old recordings—but the mood was not the same. It no longer pressed against me the way it had in years past, full of expectation and fear. Instead, it welcomed me with quiet acceptance. In that moment, I realized: music felt like home again, familiar yet new. The strings under my fingers remembered how to hum, but the melody that emerged didn't belong to the past. It belonged to my present self.

As I sat with the guitar resting gently on my lap, I closed my eyes and let the silence settle around me. There was no pressure, no ticking clock, no promise of applause, just a breath, a moment, a feeling. The first chord I strummed was soft, tentative. It wavered slightly, but it landed. And as that note echoed in the empty room, I felt something inside shift. This return wasn't about proving anything. I came back not to chase validation or approval, but to reclaim a voice that had been waiting patiently under dust, pain, and time. I realized then that I could choose my own pace instead of chasing anyone else's expectations.

I let the guitar rest against my knee and allowed myself to breathe in that sense of freedom. The rhythms of life, bills, routines, and responsibilities still existed outside the studio, quietly waiting for my attention.

But here, inside those walls, I made a vow: I would no longer let deadlines dictate my creativity. I would write when inspiration arrived, rest when my body asked, and pause when doubt whispered.

Once more, the act of creating became a process of gentleness and honesty rather than a matter of urgency or ambition. The joy was not found in the loudness of a crowd's cheering but in the stillness of the strings vibrating under one's fingers, in the gentle noise of a tune that was coming from both memory and heart.

I remembered what it felt like to chase success with a hungry, impatient heart. Back then, I believed that tracks, tours, and recognition were proof of talent. Standing here now with all the scars, past and lessons learned, I somehow sense the strength built slowly, invisibly, from within by the adversity.

Every heartbreak, every season of silence, every time I walked away from the microphone for my own sanity: those weren't failures. They were shaping. They were tempering. And as I held the guitar again, I felt that strength blooming again. I saw the resilience I had honed before fame ever touched my name, before applause ever reached my ears.

Walking slowly, not rushing chords or structure, I began to redefine what success meant. It was no longer about charts, crowds, or validation. Success became clarity, clarity of purpose, and clarity of self. It meant writing songs that echoed truth, even if I was the only one who ever heard them. Success came to mean inner alignment, honesty over hype, and meaning over metrics. When I laid down tracks again, I listened not for a spike in streams but for integrity in the tone. Not for a viral reach, but for resonance with memory, with vulnerability, with human heart.

In the days that followed, I recorded not for fans, but for myself. I pressed record, closed my eyes, and sang quietly—my voice unpolished but authentic. I recorded under dim light, leaning into nostalgia and hope, letting broken chords bloom into something fragile and new. I didn't sign the release forms. I didn't post teasers. I didn't drum up hype. I simply documented existence. I honored the voice that had survived silence. Furthermore, in those early attempts, I found a melody deeper than fame—a song made from survival, truth, and rediscovered purpose. Truly aligned.

Under soft lamplight, I strummed slowly, fingers gentle on the frets, and remembered the little girl who first touched these strings. She was full of dreams, of long nights scribbling lyrics, of hopeful chords carved in the pages of her notebook. She believed in melodies even when the world was silent.

I felt her in every tender note.

I felt her hope in my breath.

I held her innocence not as a liability, but as the foundation for everything I had become.

I showed her my respect by allowing her, once more, the opportunity to fulfill her dream—this time with maturity, prudence, and kindness as the new elements in the equation.

And I honored the woman I am now, the one who lost faith, walked through storms of doubt, and still refused to disappear. I honored the survival, the pause, the healing. I honored the nights spent wrestling with pain rather than chords, the mornings waking to responsibilities rather than rehearsals. I honored the growth that emerged not from stages, but from pain, from patience, from inner work. This return to music was not a rewind. It was a reawakening, rooted in self-discovery, in scars turned into strength, and in a wounded heart that learned how to beat again.

With each new lyric and chord, I recognized that resilience was my greatest instrument. It didn't shimmer under spotlights. It didn't promise glamour. It simply endured. It remembered. It carried forward. When a verse trembled under memory, or a chord cracked under emotion, resilience held the line. It tolerated imperfections—not as defects, but as evidence that the song was living, imperfect, and human. That weakness transformed into a connection linking the past with the present—pain with hope—silence with voice.

I recorded a song late one night, just me and dim strings, my breath steady, hands calm. When the playback came, I closed my eyes and listened. The chord carried memory, the melody carried tears, the lyrics carried scars—but underneath, there was a pulse: slow, enduring, true. That moment felt like coming home. It was familiar, but changed. Familiar in its sound, new in its heart. The same guitar, the same strings, but a different person strumming. A voice reclaimed. A soul returned.

As I tuned up once more, I understood that I had reshaped the meaning of success for myself. I no longer judged my value by audience size or streaming statistics. Instead, I defined it through clarity: clarity of purpose, clarity of truth, and clarity in choosing to remain. I found success in inner resonance, in being at peace with who I am, and in the alignment between my music and its deeper meaning.

I measured it in authenticity. When I pressed my ear to the speaker, I didn't listen for cheers. I listened for honesty.

I listened for a voice.

I listened for a home.

Music felt like home again, not because it promised fame, but because it gave me shelter. I no longer craved the spotlight. What I needed were quiet chords in gentle light, strings vibrating with memory, and lyrics shaped by survival. I needed to create not for attention, but for renewal. And so I composed gently. I recorded softly. I sang quietly. I reopened the door to my heart, unlocked it with patience, and stepped inside.

This return didn't erase the years of detour. It didn't undo the silence. It didn't pretend pain didn't exist. Instead, it acknowledged every scar, addressed every ache, and wove it into song. I embraced my story in its entirety, both the light and the darkness. I reshaped those experiences, carried them with me, and made them my own. My music no longer aimed to display perfection. It became a testament to survival, to voice, and to a life fully lived.

And in that acceptance, I found peace—not the kind that ends storms, but the kind that quiets the sea inside. I strummed chords and let their echoes settle into calm. I sang each lyric and allowed the pain to soften into sound. I breathed through the melody and felt myself rise, not because the world was listening, but because I was.

Standing at this threshold, guitar in hand, I don't rush.

I don't chase.

I don't demand.

I create.

I listen.

I heal.

I return.

Because I know now: My rhythm belongs to me.

Honoring Every Version Of Me

When I cradle the guitar in my hands these days, I carry more than strings and wood.

I carry memory.

I carry every version of me who ever believed in melody, even when silence threatened.

I carry the little girl whose fingers once trembled over her first chord, wide-eyed and hopeful, untouched by fear, believing that a handful of notes could travel beyond the walls of her room.

That child's innocence was never naïve. It was bold, defiant hope. I honor her not by reaching back for a vanished purity, but by rooting every new chord in the courage she gave me at the very beginning. Her trembling hands, her open heart—they are roots from which everything else has grown.

That early hope would have meant very little if it had never been tested by reality. So I also honor the young woman I became through dark and turbulent seasons, the one who encountered betrayal, carried grief, and endured injustice.

When every door closed, when microphones seemed silent, when applause faded into emptiness—she stayed. She did not vanish.

She did not surrender.

Instead, she learned what pain can do: it burns at edges, it grinds the soul, but it births a different kind of fire.

She carried scars no audience ever witnessed.

She patched broken strings, erased revival hopes stained by doubt, held breath until hopelessness softened, and pressed on.

I honor her by letting truth live in every note I play, by allowing each lyric to speak to survival, and by shaping harmonies that show how even scars can become sources of strength.

Between those echoes, innocence formed by hope and resilience built through survival, stands the artist I chose not to leave behind.

When everything around urged silence, she whispered back: "Sing."

She carried more than songs. She brought a story. Not polished, not perfect—raw, vulnerable, and honest.

On nights of exhaustion, days drained of creativity, in the absence of audience or expectation—she returned.

She pressed record in empty rooms, strummed chords in muted corners, hummed melodies into damp air, letting sorrow and longing shape sound.

She endured.

She waited.

She remembered that art is not only about stage lights or applause—sometimes it grows in scars turned to lyrics, pain turned to rhythm, loss turned to melody.

I honor her by letting imperfection breathe in my music.

I refuse to sanitize the past.

I allow broken strings to hum their own ache, letting truth resonate louder than polish.

Now, stepping into this chapter of return, I walk with clarity I never had before. I no longer move toward the spotlight or loud applause. I walk toward purpose. I don't ask whether I'm good enough for the industry.

I ask: Am I honest?

Am I real?

Am I living my truth?

I no longer record to prove anything. I record to speak honestly. I no longer step on stage to chase attention. I perform so the message can be felt, heart to heart, not crowd to ego. In that change, I take back more than my instrument. I take back my integrity.

I have redefined success on my own terms. It is no longer the applause of crowded halls, nor viral moments or chart positions. Success has slowed down for me. It is waking without dread, picking up the strings without pressure, and strumming gently in quiet rooms. Success is writing lyrics that shake with honesty, even if only one other soul ever hears them. Success is closing a worn notebook with verses soaked in memory, not perfect lines shaped by demand. It is breathing through melody, knowing that scars don't necessarily silence—sometimes they deepen sound, deepen meaning, and deepen connection.

This resurrection does not rely on wiping out history. It depends on acceptance of all the stages—the optimistic start, the suffering diversion, the quiet pause, and the unwelcome comeback. In each chord I play now, I trace those lines: innocence, struggle, endurance, hope. I give space for softness and strength in equal measure. I let breath carry memory. I let fingers trace scars. I let voice carry both doubt and trust. I realize that the imperfections I once judged now create texture. They don't blemish—they deepen. They give my music a soul.

So I play again on a rainy night beneath dim light, the guitar resting gently against my knee, cables still, the microphone quiet, and memory awake. I do not wait for applause. I do not rush toward release. I press record for myself.

For the little girl whose fingers first trembled.

For the young woman who survived silence.

For the artist who refused invisibility.

For the voice that remembered rhythm when all else was still.

I do not search for perfection. I invite truth. I strum softly. I exhale. I let the chord echo with history.

When the final note dissolves, and the playback hum fills the empty room, I close my eyes. I listen not for criticism or approval, but for resonance. I feel the vibration beneath my skin, the echo in my chest, and the pulse carried through memory. That resonance is not a roar. It's a hum of homecoming. A quiet hymn of return. A soft echo of resilience. In that hum, I realize: I have never lost my voice. I only lost my way. And now I'm found.

I open my eyes. I see cables coiled neatly, microphones resting, empty walls stretching outward. But I also see a possibility. In that space—once a stage of pressure, now a sanctuary of rebirth—I sense beginnings, not endings. I no longer feel pressure calling me forward, only quiet openings. There is ease where expectations once lived. The strings are familiar beneath my hands, yet I am changed. I am here not to justify my presence, but to finally feel at home.

I place my hand over the guitar's neck and whisper a vow. Not a vow of fame. Not a plea for applause.

A vow of truth.

A vow to self.

A vow to carry this journey—every part of it—forward, chord by chord.

I commit to honoring what I remember, accepting what has marked me, and respecting who I have become. I choose to sing not out of obligation to the world, but because my heart still knows the song. I choose patience, truth, and the courage to remain fully human.

That moment marks a quiet victory. A soft triumph. A reclamation. I close the session, pack away cables, rest the mic, and step into the night air. The stars overhead may not change—but I am different. Grounded. Whole. Not because everything has healed. Not because all wounds are gone. But because I have returned. I have reclaimed. I have found my voice again.

As I walk away with a guitar in hand, I don't carry expectation. I carry memory. I carry resilience. I carry purpose. I carry the little girl who first dared to dream. The young woman who survived storms. The artist who never accepted silence. I carry a story—raw, wounded, hopeful, and alive. I carry hope braided with scars. I carry rhythm—not borrowed applause, not borrowed acclaim, but forged in struggle, shaped by time, tempered by truth.

My journey does not end here. I know storms may rise again. Doubt may visit at dawn. Silence may stretch long. But I have learned what returning through silence means. I have learned that the voice does not vanish when the noise fades.

It waits.

It rests.

It regathers strength in breath, in patience, in survival.

And when the moment returns, when the strings quietly summon me again, I will lean in, lift the guitar, press record, and sing. Not because anyone asks me to. Because I remember. Because this is where I truly belong.

Because in the end, what matters is not perfection. It is perseverance. Not fame. But honesty. Not applause. But truth. Not spotlight. But heartbeat.

And as long as breath flows in my lungs and strings hum under my touch, I will play.

I will live. I will return. I will belong.

www.ingramcontent.com/pod-product-compliance
Lightning Source LLC
Chambersburg PA
CBHW071731120626
46550CB00002B/478